More Praise for
True Grit

"What an honor that these incredibly successful women give you an inside look at their lives and personal stories. If you are looking for inspiration for your career, knowing each of these remarkable women, I promise that you need to look no further."

–Rob Carter, Executive Vice President, FedEx Information Services, CIO, FedEx Corporation

"As an executive and mother of four, I understand the tenacity, confidence and courage that women must demonstrate to advance. Grab your pen and highlighter because this book may be the most useful resource you find on your personal path to success."

–Brie Carere, Executive Vice President, Chief Marketing and Communications Officer, FedEx Corporation

"If you are looking for the tools you will need for your career, look no further. True Grit provides you with inspiration and the opportunity to learn from the very best."

–Juan N. Cento, Regional President, FedEx Express, Latin America & Caribbean

"A special collection of life's learnings, converted into leadership principles by a talented group of executives — a truly incredible read."

–Dan Mullally, Senior Vice President, Sales, FedEx Services

True Grit

Stories from FedEx female leaders

Passion, Pursuit, Perseverance

Edie Hand & Jane Amaba

Copyright 2020 FedEx. All rights reserved.

First Edition: August 2020

ISBN: 978-0-578-73747-8

Printed in the United States of America

The advice and strategies found within may not be suitable for every situation. This work is sold with the understanding that neither the authors nor the publisher is held responsible for the results accrued from the advice in this book.

Without limiting the rights under the copyright reserved above, no part of this publication may be reproduced, distributed, transmitted, stored or introduced into a retrieval system in any form or by any means, including photocopying, recording, or other electronic or mechanical methods, without the prior written permission of the publisher.

FedEx Corporate Services, Inc.
3620 Hacks Cross Road, Memphis, Tennessee 38125

TrueGrit@corp.ds.fedex.com

www.fedex.com

FedEx and the FedEx logo are registered marks and Roxo and FedEx SameDay Bot are marks of Federal Express Corporation or one of its affiliates. Women of True Grit is a registered mark of The Edie Hand Foundation.

Photo credit: Edie Hand's photo by Josh Fogel

The Story of a Pearl

Most people have at some time heard about how a pearl is created. A pearl forms when a piece of grit slips between the mantle and the shell of an oyster. The grit irritates the mantle and the oyster coats the grit – layer by layer – with nacre (mother-of-pearl) in order to protect itself. After enough layers, a beautiful pearl forms from what was originally grit.

Just like the oyster, each woman whose story is told in this book has her own grit which she has layered with her life experiences and challenges to become the woman she is.

Each one is a unique pearl. Just as we all are.

We hope these stories inspire you. As you read each example of grit and determination, and the pearls of wisdom created, reflect on your own story and how your experiences have made you the unique pearl that you are.

Table of Contents

Acknowledgements .... *viii*

Introduction .... *ix*

Cathy Ross *1*

Rebecca Yeung *7*

Marilyn Blanco-Reyes *12*

Lisa Lisson *18*

Kawal Preet *23*

Bobbi Wells *29*

Gloria Roberts Boyland *35*

Tracci Schultz *40*

Captain Cheryl Pitzer *46*

Suzanne Garber *51*

Ramona Hood *57*

Jill Brannon *61*

Peggy Carrera *66*

Jane Amaba *72*

Gina Adams *78*

Karen Reddington *84*

Aimee DiCicco-Ruhl *89*

Acknowledgments

Throughout this book you will see references to Quality Driven Management, or QDM, which is fundamental to how work is completed at FedEx. One of the six pillars of QDM is 'Quality Involves Teamwork,' which is well proven in the production of this book.

Thank you to all who played a key part in delivering our final product:

Dan Mullaly- An inspiring leader and avid supporter of diversity and inclusion, whose introduction of Jane to Edie set in motion a partnership to enrich and inspire women.

Michele Ehrhart- A powerful storyteller, whose vision in what this book could be was the inspiration to start this journey, and whose magical use of words and editing could pull out stories from those who were humble and reluctant to believe their stories were worth telling.

Amy Clunan- A dedicated attorney whose partnership from the beginning was instrumental in achieving this final product recapping the journeys of FedEx female leaders through times requiring grit to the unique pearls of leaders they have become.

Amy Feehan- A visionary writer, whose input through the review process transformed many stories to more purposefully call out pearls of wisdom and be a playbook for personal growth.

Aaron Petty- An amazing and talented graphic artist who took ownership of our manuscript and devoted significant time to pull together a fantastic finished product.

Steve Hays- A knowledgeable print product manager whose patience and knowledge directed many of the decisions in this publication.

Katherine Newsom Pierotti- A gifted designer whose front cover design, featuring a pearl necklace, was the inspiration for the pearl theme throughout this publication.

Rebecca Janes- A creative designer whose proposal for a story template with a space for personal notes on each story, was pivotal in rethinking the look and feel of this book.

Lauren Smith- A talented creator, who blended various ideas into a story template foundational to this publication.

Lauren Doll, Audrey Evensky Brantz, Margaret Atkinson Martin, Rachel Wolfson, Helena Orgeron- AP Style gurus and editors who reviewed these stories.

Tammy Mailhot and Holly Pate- Supporters of Women in Leadership whose partnership helped in the final review before printing.

Joyce Charity Ware- Administrator of the consolidation point for document sharing.

And of course, to all of the remarkable female leaders who shared their personal stories to give readers examples of perseverance and determination to overcome challenges and achieve their dreams and goals.

Introduction

The mission of Women in Leadership (WIL) is to drive action and strategy to advance FedEx Services' objectives by engaging the communities we serve, enriching women's personal and professional growth, empowering women to contribute to our company's success while elevating women in leadership and excellence in the workplace. We strive to connect women with possibilities through purposeful events, education and engagement opportunities always looking for new ways to build our future leaders.

When I started discussing this project, the goal was to provide inspiration to women in times of challenge. The project kicked off right after a celebration of International Women's Day in early March of 2020. I never imagined that one-week later life as we knew it would change. COVID-19 certainly provided challenges that no one expected and certainly could not plan for. It made this project more important than ever.

From the beginning, the hardest part of this project was to identify which of the amazing and inspirational leaders would be the first to be included. As the demands of running a business in the midst of a global pandemic escalated, the featured stories represent those who I know well enough to relentlessly pursue in this time of crisis. They have such a strong passion for mentoring and inspiring women that even a worldwide virus couldn't get in the way of making time to contribute by telling their stories.

"True Grit, Stories of FedEx female leaders" is a collection of stories from women who grew up in small towns and achieved their goals and dreams building their careers with an organization that is consistently ranked among the world's most admired and trusted companies.

This is where you come in. If we want to see the number of women in leadership grow, we need to share our own experiences. This book does just that. You will read stories of amazing female leaders who share a part of themselves so that each of you may learn and grow. Candor takes bravery which is a trait of true leadership. The women in this book serve as shining examples of leaders who have accepted challenges, overcome obstacles and persevered to meet their personal and professional goals.

I challenge you to use this book as a guide to help continue the conversation. Make it a priority to mentor others and share your own stories as ways to keep investing and cultivating in the leaders of tomorrow.

Enjoy!

Jane Amaba
Executive Sponsor for FedEx Women in Leadership

" There is a solution to every problem. "
- Unknown

" Nobody, but nobody can make it out here alone. "
- Maya Angelou

Cathy

Ross

Retired
Executive Vice President and CFO
FedEx Express

True grit is determination, survival and courageously driving forward when life is rough and the future unknown.

I was raised on a farm with a strong work ethic instilled in us by parents who made certain we were focused on being the best we could be — no excuses.

My mother was a teacher and my father a farmer who had to work in a factory to make ends meet. My parents had tried to have children but finally gave up and adopted my sister. As so often happens, my mother became pregnant and I came along less than a year later. My sister, Gloria, and I never doubted how much we were cherished or how determined our parents were that we would become productive, civic-minded, caring Christian adults. Achievement was simply part of the fabric of our lives.

We were not wealthy, and we knew what hard work was. We chopped and picked cotton, drove the tractor, milked cows, tended the garden, canned meats and vegetables, cooked, cleaned and whatever else had to be done. In high school, I won the Betty Crocker award, received academic achievement honors and was in just about every club, newspaper or group there was.

In the 4-H club, one of my projects was to raise 100 baby chicks. The problem was I was terrified of chickens — and still am. I did it because my parents maintained that it built character when you faced and overcame your fears. That was about the time I realized that I was not cut out to be a farmer, so I decided I would go to college as my parents expected. Over the years, some white people have asked if I was a teacher or a nurse, as that was their expectation for the highest job a Black person who presented themselves as I do could have — there aren't many who look like me in executive roles.

My parents were savers and achievers. They bought a farm only a few years after getting married, and starting their lives together as sharecroppers. Mom was valedictorian of her class although she had to leave home and live with another family to be able to attend high school. There were no Black high schools close to her home and attending a white school was not an option for her in those days. She started teaching at 18, even before she earned her college degree, then became one of the first African American teachers to integrate the school system in our county. Of course, she took my sister and me along with her, making us among the first Black students at what had been all-white schools. My mother's mantra was "Go! Go to church, go to school and go to work."

I remember racial segregation very well. We had to sit in the balcony at the movies, couldn't go inside most restaurants and had to be aware of white-only signs on water fountains and restrooms. When we took road trips, we packed our own food because there was uncertainty about where we could get served. My father was as self-sufficient as possible. He did not want to have to depend on the uncertainty of the prejudices we might encounter. That doesn't mean that our community was bad. We were all farmers — Black and white — and most people had similar values and challenges and pitched in to help each other. We depended a lot, however, on our close family and good friends.

Our close family was a large one. There were 23 grandchildren and eight siblings on my father's side and 15 grandchildren and four siblings on my mother's side. Most of them lived nearby, and we spent a lot of time together with our bunch of cousins. From that group has come a great deal of achievement despite the challenges of poverty and racial discrimination. I attribute this to our small-town values — work hard, have high ethics, be honest, live by the Golden Rule, respect others, do all you can with what you've been given, help others, respect yourself and serve the community in a way that would make everyone proud.

By the time I went to college in 1975, Blacks had more opportunities. I received a full scholarship and went to a small college with an excellent academic reputation and values I appreciated. I was very active in campus life and graduated with a degree in accounting in three years — at the age of 20.

Things always work out better if you take ownership of your problem and try to find a solution.

Upon graduation, I went to work at a subsidiary of Proctor & Gamble Company, where I quickly was promoted into a management position. I also started studying for my MBA degree with an eye on financial analysis. To me, that focus allowed me to set my sights on the future, not just report on the past. During my first day on the job, my manager shared something that stayed with me. He simply said, "Solve your own problems." I was not totally sure what he meant. It even sounded a bit harsh. I have since realized things always work out better if you take ownership of your problem and try to find a solution. You can always ask for help if you can't fix it. But first, get about doing it.

Next, I joined Kimberly-Clark as a cost analyst and again moved into a management position in just over a year. I had college friends who were at FedEx and loved it. When my next promotion at Kimberly-Clark would have required me to relocate far from my family, I instead joined FedEx as a senior financial analyst. I never intended to stay for 30 years, but it was so rewarding the time flew by. I was executive vice president and CFO of FedEx Express when I retired. I once calculated I either changed jobs, got promoted or had some other significant change in my role at FedEx every 1.3 years.

Life has not always been easy, and I have learned the meaning of true grit to get through the toughest of times. My sister died in a car accident at the age of 29. She left a husband and 4-year-old child. Losing Gloria changed my life forever. I threw myself into my work because I could not bear to think about living without her. She was a bright ray of sunshine, and her loss was like turning out a light that left me in deep darkness. Everything I had been taught in my life came to bear. I was more focused, driven and achievement-oriented than ever.

When I joined FedEx, the company was growing so fast that the ability to think quickly, work hard and take on new challenges was rewarded. I learned a lot very quickly and was given opportunities that kind of situation offered. I built relationships at all levels within the company and became known as someone who would take the initiative and solve problems. That led to new, evolving roles for me in finance supporting nearly every division of FedEx and ultimately to my position as executive vice president and CFO of FedEx Express.

The work ethic and values instilled in me by my parents were drivers of my career — not reaching a certain level or promotion. I was more interested in learning and excelling in whatever I was doing. As a result of that, and the trust-based relationships I had built, the promotions came. I worked hard, kept my word, did my best, and treated others as I wanted to be treated. I never asked anyone to do what I wouldn't do. I was honest and forthright and tried to set the example.

I was a successful leader because I appreciated the value of people regardless of their abilities or circumstances. I believed in the importance of making connections at every level and across the globe. It wasn't always easy with 5,000 employees around the world in the FedEx Express Finance organization; yet, I wanted every individual to feel part of something bigger, and I wanted them to know what they needed to do to excel. It is not unlike meeting our parents' expectations growing up. People, regardless of where they live, need to know what is expected of them and have a personal connection to each other and to their leaders. I often said, "There aren't bad employees. They are just in the wrong job. It is our role as leaders to help them find a spot in which they can succeed."

I tried to visit each region at least once a year and hold town halls in major facilities. It was often the first time that employees had ever seen an executive. And, in some places, the first time meeting a person of color. I made sure to go to every employee's workstation, have a short conversation, shake their hand and look them directly in the eye. In some locations — like Wuhan, China — where there were over 500 employees, I needed an interpreter and it took hours.

I especially liked connecting personally through pictures of families, pets or other things displayed in workspaces. Though I felt the cultural differences, I was reminded that inside we are all the same. We all care about our families, want to provide for them, care about how we are perceived by others and desire to be treated fairly. We may all have different roles to play, but ultimately, we are all in this together. Real strength comes from accepting our differences and pulling together. After all, we are all human and deserving of dignity.

Through the years, my resume has grown with a number of prestigious "labels." I won FedEx's highest honors — the Five Star and CEO Awards — seven times. I received numerous awards from external organizations and was featured in the press. I was the first African American executive vice president, first African American vice president in Financial Planning, and first female or African American in several other roles. Our society can be quick to label, but I never labeled myself as a "female" or "African American." Instead, I am a capable businessperson, a caretaker, an optimist, a torch bearer and a problem solver. And that is how I want people to "label" and remember me.

I want to be recognized as a woman of grace. Someone who may have been flawed and uniquely human, but a person who acknowledged those flaws and worked hard to correct them. And along the way, I encouraged others to do the same. Many do not realize that I am shy. I often have a hard time thinking of what to say, and I have a terrible memory for names. Like many shy people, deep down, I am afraid I won't be accepted and that others around me will be much more confident and interesting than me. I had to work at being an extrovert by recognizing situations where I would be uncomfortable and then preparing myself, often in advance. I've always admired people, like my sister, who could strike up a conversation with anyone. She had a set of five questions she would ask to encourage people to engage. I now use them. The funny thing is that now after many years of practice, when I take personality tests, I am labeled as an extrovert. But I still have to take a deep breath when I go into a room full of strangers.

I have learned through years of leadership and growth that we can all benefit from constructive criticism and evaluation. Being open to and seeking the honest input of others is one of the best opportunities to grow and improve. I will never forget an event where I had a conversation with a bright and capable female manager in my organization. I noticed she ended each statement with a nervous giggle. I am not usually so blunt, but I asked her if she was aware that she was doing it. She was naturally taken aback, and I wondered if I should have mentioned it. I told her I was going to set up a meeting with her so we could talk. Later, she told me she went home that night and asked her husband if she giggled. He told her she did and it made her appear to lack confidence. She and I met once a month and discussed her demonstration of confidence, leadership, career plan and more. She has done very well at the company and is now an officer. I take no credit for her accomplishments. She deserves all of them because she worked hard for the company and, at the same time, on herself.

If I had to do one thing differently, it would be to stop and smell the roses. I missed opportunities to spend good times with friends or family because I thought I was too busy. I have learned taking more time to have fun with others can make a person better overall. That's why I planned my retirement based on the "Five Fs," which I heard from a friend. She suggested devoting my newfound free time to faith, family, fun, finances and fitness. It would be the first time in my life I had not been directly responsible for anything except my own happiness, and I wanted to make the most of it. My mother had a stroke just before I retired, giving me the opportunity to spend precious time with her in her last years. I remember the time I proudly called my mother to recount all the things I had accomplished on my to-do list that day. She listened and then told me in retirement I could not measure success by doing a bunch of little things. What would matter would be doing the big things — things that could change lives. She was right, and I often hear her words as I plan how I am going to use my time.

True grit is determination, survival and courageously driving forward when life is rough and the future unknown. It is like being a little Black girl growing up in a segregated world. It is courage to overcome fear, like taking care of those baby chicks in 4-H Club. It is perseverance, prevailing even when you lose the brightest light in your life, as I did twice. First, it was the sudden death of my sister. The other was when I had to make the decision to let my precious mother go to palliative care rather than keep fighting the doctors in the hopeless effort to keep her alive.

True Grit is at the core of all of us.

I am more convinced than ever that true grit is at the core of all of us. We are born with it, but we so often fail to use it when we need it the most. Sometimes we just have to reach down deep within ourselves, find it and put it to good use. As my mother said so often, we just need to grab it and "Go!"

What details or lessons in this story resonate with me? And why?

How will I apply what I read or learned to my own career or personal life?

" Some failure in life is inevitable. It is impossible to live without failing at something, unless you live so cautiously that you might as well not have lived at all — in which case, you fail by default. "
- J.K. Rowling

Rebecca

Yeung

Vice President,
Advanced Technology
and Innovation
FedEx Corporation

True grit is the ability and willingness to take risks, persevere when things get rough and stick to goals until they are realized. Because of my unique childhood and background, I had many opportunities to develop and practice internal strength.

I was born in China during the height of the Cultural Revolution when there was very little freedom, and the government could tell anyone where to go, where to live and what to do for a living. My parents were assigned jobs in two different cities where they each made about $12 a month. Unable to afford a nanny, they made the difficult and heartbreaking decision to send me to live with my aunt in her tiny rural village.

Without electricity or running water, we relied on a single oil lamp for light and a bucket of water drawn and carried from a well. The house in which we lived had dirt floors. Even so, I never thought of myself as being poor because everyone else in the village lived the same way. There were no schools, and we did not have toys to play with. However, my friends and I always managed to find fun things to do. The truth is, I was building grit at a young age, learning to make the most of any situation. Except for being hungry, I really enjoyed my early childhood. I remember always being curious, anxious to learn and try new things, even though there was no formal education available.

When I was seven years old, my mother and I were allowed to move to Shanghai, the same place where my father lived and worked. While it was wonderful to have my family reunited, it was also a difficult transition because I went from being very social and knowing everyone to being an outsider. Since I came from a village with no schooling, I was an easy target and often picked on by others.

> True grit is the ability and willingness to take risks, persevere when things get rough and stick to goals until they are realized.

On my first day of school, I did not know the alphabet or even how to write my own name. The city kids looked down on me.

My mom, who was a huge influence and mentor in my life, helped me through the transition. I remember one pep talk particularly. She told me that I had two choices: I could accept the way the other kids were treating me, or I could stand up and defend myself. Even after 40 years, I think back on that big decision for a little girl. I became a fighter. I made it my goal to catch up and even surpass my peers in the classroom. After I graduated as the top student in my high school, I was accepted at a prestigious Chinese university. I went on to receive a degree in English and began my career as a consultant for a British company.

It did not take long to discover significant pay inequality at my first job. This hard reality was a big milestone because it forced me to take a risk both personally and professionally. I was not going to settle after having come so far. I had heard about something called "the American Dream" when I was growing up. I had always been fascinated by the concept, even before I had any idea of what it meant. If I was going to experience that dream, I would need to set my sights on the United States of America.

With hard work and determination, I received a scholarship from the University of Maryland to attend its MBA program. I had $100 in cash and packed everything I owned in luggage. But it all paled in comparison to the last hurdle I had to overcome before I left China — saying goodbye to my father. He went with me to the airport and begged me not to leave. He was deeply worried about his only child going to a foreign country, more than 7,000 miles away, without friends or family. I was so eager to start a new life that nothing could have stopped me at that point. Now that I am a mother myself, I have a newfound appreciation for my father's concerns, the profound love he has for me and the freedom he gave me to fly off to pursue my dream.

I discovered a lot of mental strength and courage in my move so far from home and family. In those days, international telephone calls were very expensive, so I rarely got to talk to my mom and dad. I did not get to see my parents for three years. Though it was difficult to get through the separation, it helped that my parents took so much pride in my academic and professional accomplishments. More than anything else, they were proud of my courage to take that giant leap and strike out on my own.

When I first arrived in Maryland, I did not fit in. I remembered the advice my mom gave me when I faced the transition to Shanghai. I had not fit in there either. So, I did exactly what I did back then. I worked incredibly hard and learned to adjust to the new environment by overcoming language barriers and cultural differences. My MBA internship was with the Strategic Market Analysis department at FedEx. The company was one of several to offer me a position after I graduated, but I chose FedEx because I liked the focus on people. When I moved to Memphis, my plan was to stay with the company for a couple of years, learn all I could, and then move on. But now, almost 20 years later, I am still proud to be a part of this great company.

I didn't become a manager at FedEx until I was almost 40 — a bit late for many who aspire to corporate leadership. But that did not deter my dream. Throughout my early career at FedEx, I never stopped building up a huge repository of essential business skills and knowledge about FedEx operations. I worked hard to understand all aspects of the business from emerging technology to operations, customer experience, strategic planning and analysis. That time spent gaining experience and increasing responsibility proved to be tremendously helpful as I advanced at FedEx and ultimately led to an officer position — a level very few Asian females have reached. One of my career highlights is driving enterprise wide adoption of Quality Driven Management (QDM) and making it part of everything we do at FedEx. Now as vice president of Advanced Technology and Innovation, I am responsible for leading autonomous vehicles and robotics initiatives to help the enterprise achieve a higher level of efficiency and an improved customer experience.

Many ask how someone with a degree in English and an MBA is now leading initiatives in the STEM field. The secret sauce centers on continued learning and willingness to take on new risks. The fear of failure often unnerves a person from trying new opportunities, but to me, life becomes far more fascinating when you can tackle a completely new field and excel in it. With focus on continual learning and building experience throughout my career, I have acquired an incredible amount of expertise in advanced technologies which enabled me to lead in this new space, including the prototyping of Roxo™, the FedEx SameDay bot.

No doubt, my career was built on the foundation of my childhood dreams. But dreams shouldn't stop at a certain age. At any stage of life, it is important to maintain a clear vision of goals, where you want to be, what you want to accomplish. And with time and experience, those goals can continue to evolve. I tell my team that it is hard to live a dream unless you begin by visualizing and articulating what you want to accomplish. When someone asks me what it takes for a woman to excel in a male-dominated environment, I tell them to set goals, lean in, be prepared and have a seat at the table. Be confident and positive by focusing on opportunities, not barriers, building on your strengths instead of focusing on your weaknesses.

Throughout my career at FedEx, I have also recognized the importance of teamwork. I have had the privilege of working with amazing individuals and built incredible teams. I am most gratified professionally when I can challenge and energize a person or group to achieve goals or their best work. I am not one of those people who wants all the credit. I would much prefer leading a team to accomplish great things, helping them develop and grow. I am so proud that in the last five years, four of my direct reports reached the next level of their careers.

> **Be confident and positive by focusing on opportunities, not barriers, building on your strengths instead of focusing on your weaknesses.**

In today's fast-paced climate, one of the most significant lessons I have learned is to maintain a balance between work and family life. That includes developing a personal compass to guide my decisions based on all aspects of my life. I am blessed to have married my husband, Kevin. In 20 years of marriage, he has been and continues to be my rock. He has given me unwavering support for my career. We have two daughters. I am particularly proud to teach them about their Chinese heritage. Several years ago, I had the opportunity to return to the village where I grew up. I took my daughters with me so they could experience the beauty and the challenges of rural China for themselves. It was important to show them where my journey started and to inspire the confidence in them to pursue their own dreams without giving up.

An important part of balance extends beyond the walls of business. One of my personal priorities is giving back to the community. When my girls and I were in the village in China, it brought back many memories, including how it feels to be hungry. Even in one of the world's wealthiest nations, families and — more importantly — children are so often food insecure. I know firsthand how difficult it is for children to fight against discouragement and to dream about a better future when they are hungry. Now, I serve as a director on the board of the Mid-South Food Bank in Memphis assisting others as they fight for and dream about a better life.

There are many paths to success, so each person must define what success means to them. All of us suffer challenges and setbacks in life. All of us reach points of decision when taking a risk can change the course of our lives. Make those decisions with confidence. Hard work, determination, being prepared, perseverance and a little bit of luck will pay off. You won't be perfect, and you will make mistakes. You will be tempted to compare yourself to others and lose momentum. Yet it is often in those moments of challenge that we gain our best learning. So, live your life with enthusiasm and approach each challenge with true grit. Don't let caution cause you to default on your dreams.

What details or lessons in this story resonate with me? And why?

How will I apply what I read or learned to my own career or personal life?

Marilyn
Blanco-Reyes

Vice President, Legal & Regulatory Affairs, Latin American & Caribbean Division FedEx Express

> I understood grit to mean anybody who was tough but with a tender side beneath a rough veneer. Someone who gets the job done no matter what, but ultimately someone who has a good heart and pure intentions.

" All that a person achieves and all that he (or she) fails to achieve is a direct result of that person's own thoughts. As he (or she) thinks, so he (or she) is; as he (or she) continues to think, so he (or she) remains. "
- British writer James Allen

I remember the first time I heard the words true grit as a child in New York City in the 1970s — a few years after the John Wayne movie with that title came out. I did not know what the term meant because my English was not strong since we had just recently migrated as a family from Cuba. I understood it to mean anybody who was tough but with a tender side beneath a rough veneer. Someone who gets the job done no matter what, but ultimately someone who has a good heart and pure intentions.

Movies were important to me from an early age, especially after coming to the U.S. as a young child. My parents worked multiple jobs to put us through school, so my brother and I were often home alone and spent many hours watching New York television. The stations played lots of old black-and-white films — romances, comedies, adventures and westerns — but the romances were my favorites, just as romantic songs are my preferred type of music to this day. They were what kept us occupied in our new home and helped us learn to speak English.

My childhood began in Havana, Cuba. I remember that we lived very comfortably, a typical upper middle-class family of the time and place. Then, in the early 1960s, my family left Cuba in the wake of the Castro Revolution. In the process, we left behind everything we had. Not just property and belongings, but also my grandparents, other family members and friends. While that must have been a difficult decision, my mother and father were determined that their son and daughter would not be raised in a Communist country. Neither of our parents spoke a word of English. They had no jobs, no assets and no plan, but they were resolved to start over.

Their courage to take the risk for their family was a very memorable first lesson in true grit. Despite the difficulties they faced, they did everything they could to ensure that my brother and I experienced the American Dream. That included living in safe neighborhoods and attending great schools. They encouraged us to assimilate into American life while staying true to our Cuban traditions.

I always believed that I would be successful at whatever I chose to do in life — something my family instilled in me from early childhood. I just had no idea what that success would look like. I remember reading about the Nobel Peace prize and thinking, "Hmmm, that would be cool to get one day." I set high expectations for myself, and I still encourage others to do the same.

When my family moved to Miami, I went to an all-girls Catholic school. We were required to wear a uniform to class each day and makeup was not allowed. I may have fussed at the time, but I soon realized that these rules gave us an amazing amount of freedom, not having to worry about trying to dress to impress each other or making an impression on boys. We all dressed the same, regardless of family backgrounds, making it easier to concentrate on our studies and not what we wore. The camaraderie there was unique, too. While many resented the strictness and high expectations, I loved it. The high bar and experiences at school instilled the importance of being well prepared in everything we did. That includes the right level of education, the proper training and diverse real-world experiences. If we are prepared and have done the work to get ready, we can then proceed with confidence into any situation.

> **If we are prepared and have done the work to get ready, we can then proceed with confidence into any situation.**

I was immersed in a bi-cultural, bi-lingual environment at a young age, becoming more and more aware of different cultures and lifestyles. One thing that stood out to me from the beginning was the difference in what my classmates and I brought from home for lunch each day. The other kids had their bologna or peanut butter and jelly sandwiches. I typically brought traditional Cuban fare, such as arroz con pollo. But nobody made fun of me. We happily shared and learned just a little bit more about each other, our differences and our similarities, thus preparing ourselves for the real world.

As a young girl enamored with the movies and Hollywood, I decided that I wanted to be in the movie business. But not in front of the camera. Somehow, I knew the real power was behind the camera, so my dream was to be a movie director, bringing my own story and experiences to the big screen. But there was also a practical side to this dreamer, and I realized that international relations, diplomacy and ultimately, law was a better fit.

I attended Miami-Dade Community College, earning an associate degree before taking my first job with Eastern Airlines. I traveled the world while I continued my studies. I earned my bachelor's degree from Florida International University and continued to the University of Miami School of Law, where I gravitated toward international law. I was recruited by a Brazilian law firm and worked in São Paulo for two years. I made friends and fell in love with the country. It is a love affair that continues today. Later, I went to work for FedEx and helped open the company's Latin America and Caribbean regional legal office in Brazil. After five years in Brazil, the company brought me back to Miami, where I was once again near my family with access to interesting people and locales.

Today, as a female executive, I look for ways to positively influence other women and minorities. You see, I am a member of four minority groups, three of which I happily represent and one I am not quite ready to accept so gracefully. I am a woman. I am Hispanic. I am gay. But the last one — crossing into that senior age bracket — is something I'm still working on.

My parents, and my extended family, have always been the touchstone of life and my biggest fans, who have showered me with love and affection. That did not keep me from worrying about whether they would still be proud of me after I made a key decision in my life. Coming out as a gay woman is probably the easiest yet most difficult thing that I have ever done. It was easy because it was natural and pure. I knew it was the right thing to do, that I was being true to who I am. But it was so very difficult because I knew how society viewed homosexuality at the time, and I was concerned about how my parents and loved ones would react. Thankfully, I always had the loving support of my family, and that has enabled me to live a happy and fulfilled life.

I have been inspired by many people, some I knew personally and some who I have only read about or seen in the media. That includes some wonderful folks at FedEx. But easily my greatest inspiration and true mentor is my father, Gustavo. Much like the true grit definition inspired by John Wayne, my father was tough but had a tender side that my family knew well. He is an old-style Cuban gentleman, but despite his Latin machista upbringing — his strong sense of masculine pride — he always encouraged my independence and empowered me to take on challenges. His work ethic and organizational skills set a wonderful example for me and have been a key to my success. He and my mother both insisted that we always do the right thing, be true to ourselves and work hard. I will never forget taking my then 80-year-old father to the FedEx headquarters in Memphis, Tenn. I was able to get him a private tour of the hub. Anyone who has ever been to the hub knows what an amazing place it is. I could tell by the look on Dad's face that he finally understood how big this thing was that his little girl was a part of, and I could see just how proud he was.

Over the years, I've become more aware of the human rights abuses that take place all over the world. Tragedies such as the current human migration crisis in Venezuela, the abuse of LGBT rights in the Middle East and other places, the deforestation in my former home country of Brazil, and the attacks on personal freedom in China — just to name a few. I vowed to try to be a part of helping as much as I could. That includes being active in the Miami Committee of Human Rights Watch (HRW), an international, non-governmental organization dedicated to research and advocacy on human rights. The Miami Committee, which was founded in 2016, is a network of informed and engaged leaders who are dedicated to advancing human rights in our community and around the world by deepening HRW's presence in South Florida. I've been following the work of HRW for many years and admire how its investigations and reports can bring attention to human rights issues so significant and lasting changes can be made. I am also involved in Haitian causes, in Haiti and Miami, including disaster relief and pro bono legal work for individuals and families in the community.

> **We simply must take command now of what we can control or change.**

All of us can make a difference in standing up for inequity and injustice, but too many of us are afraid to "speak truth to power," afraid of losing our jobs, friends or prestige. But, if we speak respectfully and are backed with the facts, we cannot fail. We simply must take command now of what we can control or change. We cannot wait for society, our employers or our laws to create a better environment. I am not so naïve to think that we can change overnight prejudices and systems that have been in place for centuries. But, if we try to change what we can and if more people can emerge from the bonds of human suffering to lead others, change will ultimately occur.

Someone once asked me to describe myself in one sentence. Impossible. But if I had to, I would say: a Cuban American, Brazilian-wannabe and international attorney who is always curious about life and people. I love my career at FedEx, now approaching a quarter century. I lead a team that manages all the "legal" stuff that companies need to survive and succeed. But there are other aspects of our role that are rewarding as well, like the amazing growth — from acquisitions and organic — that I have seen in the Latin America and Caribbean region over the past few years. When I started with the company, we had about 2,000 people scattered throughout the Caribbean and Latin America. We now have about 25,000. In my department, where there were once only two of us, there are now 80 very busy people. And where Latin America was once only a small part of the FedEx world, we are now a big business, a major player in the region, and still growing. But it is not just about the growth of the business. Those of us with purple blood understand and work with passion for FedEx. Not just for the paycheck, but because we believe in the brand and our role in connecting the world.

> **Be more mindful of the journey instead of focusing so much on the destination.**

I am very disciplined when it comes to work, but outside work, I am very easy-going. I enjoy travel; it's a part of that long-held desire to see how the rest of the world looks and how people live. Along the way, I've learned to be more mindful of the journey instead of focusing so much on the destination. I love visiting Italy and lingering at the table for long delicious meals. I've had horseback riding vacations in Buenos Aires, Argentina, and Middleburg, Virginia. If I did not pause to look at the scenery, I would have missed a lot of wonderful people and experiences. I also love to stay home and entertain. That comes from Dad, who has always enjoyed having people over. Now in his 90s, he continues to be the life of the party. Our get-togethers with friends and family involve food and wine/rum and seem to inevitably end with music and dancing. We remain Cuban to the core!

As women, we must take ownership of creating our own futures and pursue life with "flawsome" confidence.

While I believe that everyone follows his or her destiny and I am very happy with the way that my life and career have turned out, I do sometimes wonder what would have happened if I had pursued my original dream as a movie director. I know that it was not just the impractical nature of Hollywood that sent me off in another direction. It was also that I was afraid of failing, of not being successful. I believe that many of us, particularly women, limit our dreams because focusing on our flaws leads to fears that we will not measure up. That distorted thinking is a barrier that we must identify and remove. It took me a while, but I finally realized how much more joyous life is when I am less critical and more accepting of myself. "Flawsome" is one of my favorite words: an adjective used to describe a person who embraces all of their quirks and "flaws" and realizes they are awesome regardless. As women, we must take ownership of creating our own futures and pursue life with "flawsome" confidence.

What details or lessons in this story resonate with me? And why?

How will I apply what I read or learned to my own career or personal life?

Lisa

Lisson

President,
FedEx Express Canada

True grit means setting goals, developing passion and perseverance, making a plan, showing courage and using your inner strength to accomplish the things that are important to you no matter what comes your way.

" *Resilience is that ineffable quality that allows some people to be knocked down by life and come back stronger than ever.* "
- Psychology Today

I believe true grit means setting goals, developing passion and perseverance, making a plan, showing courage and using your inner strength to accomplish the things that are important to you no matter what comes your way. That includes business goals as well as goals in your personal life. Regardless of the challenges you face, having a plan and sticking to it are essential to excelling in life. Grit is your strength of character.

We have all been told, and innately know, that we will face challenges in this life. However, none of us knows how difficult and life-altering those challenges may be. My husband Patrick, my high school sweetheart, and I were in our 30s with four children and living our best life. We both had exciting, satisfying and successful careers underway when everything changed — literally in a heartbeat. We had just returned from a family vacation that turned out to be our last. In the middle of the night, I was awakened by a heavy thump and found Patrick on the floor near the bed, unconscious and without a heartbeat. I immediately started CPR, until the emergency medical responders arrived and rushed him to the hospital.

Though he was young, in good shape and with no history of cardiac issues, he had suffered a massive heart attack. The loss of oxygen to his brain left him in a vegetative state. We had both signed living wills, expressing our desire to not be kept alive if there was no hope for living a meaningful life, which we assumed would be when we were 88, not 38. Admittedly, this was a decision I had not planned to make at this point in our lives. But I knew that pulling that lifesaving plug was irreversible. I asked the doctors if miracles ever happened in their hospital. They said, "Of course they do." So, I decided to fight for Patrick and see if we were going to get our miracle.

I wish I could tell you he got better and recovered, but that was not the case. In retrospect, I believe I made the right decision because we had two more years before he passed away. Two more years for our children — who were three, five, seven and nine at the time of his heart attack — to adjust to our new normal. I made a point of bringing Patrick home every Sunday, even though he gave no signs of knowing what was going on around him. The children and I knew he was there, and that allowed the kids to visit with him and to gradually accept the inevitable.

Most often during speaking engagements, I am asked about how I have navigated the loss of Patrick. I'm very open about sharing the journey with my husband because I can impart my firm belief that though his life was lost — and far too early — I learned to cope, identifying the good and the bad that came from it. I chose to seek out life lessons I could acquire from what was truly a horrible thing and became a stronger person because of it. I learned the meaning of true grit in those worst days of my family's lives. I learned that it's important to have a plan, but just as important to get back up when you are knocked down. I learned that true grit is about strength of character — the ability to face challenges with courage and passion and accomplish things that matter, regardless of what comes your way. I want others to know that life goes on, that we all have a choice to overcome heartbreak and hardship. My mother said to me, "Life is not about what happens to you, it's about what you choose to do with what happens." Though it is not always easy, I make a conscious decision every day to choose happiness and gratitude. Even in the darkest moments, we can find a reason to smile. It is not easy, but few things in life worth having are.

I am a big believer in focusing on the here and now — I call it living in 24-hour increments. Thinking about the past robs you of the beauty all around you, so I surround myself with people, places and things that inspire me and strive to find enjoyment in the moment. I learned the hard way that none of us knows what tomorrow brings, so we can't waste one moment of the precious gift of life.

Even the 24-hour increments require being intentional. My position demands that I practice effective time management to fulfill my duties as a business executive and also as a mother. Scheduling conflicts do come up, but that's just part of life. I am an early riser and try to be home most nights by 5:30 p.m. so I can have dinner with the family and hear about their day. I have also learned there is no such thing as the perfect work-life balance. In fact, I don't like the word "perfect." It is more about adapting to the ebb and flow of work and our personal lives and cutting ourselves some slack when things don't go according to our plans. I always say, "Tomorrow is a new day."

Though it sounds like a contradiction, we must manage our lives and calendars by building in white space both professionally and at home. Even if it represents only a couple of hours a week to relax and recharge my mind by reading a book, meeting a friend for coffee or doing yoga, the white space is good for your mind, body and soul. Including white space at work helps you refocus as well. When there are no meetings or phone calls, I take time to plan and prioritize, focusing on what has to get done and by when. Then I'll accompany my kids to things that are important to them. That makes those things important to me, too.

I also enjoy mentoring others and doing speaking engagements. Hopefully I pass along some of the things I have learned to help others achieve their goals. I am convinced that success — not just in business, but in life — is all about creating your own unique value proposition. What you can offer as a contribution to the goals of your company, or what you can bring to any relationship, gives you more worth to your employer and to the people who are important to you. That value not only gives you a better chance to advance to your dream job, or to have better relationships, but also offers tremendous personal satisfaction. That's because you know you did things the right way, that you earned what you have gotten.

With over 28 years at FedEx and multiple positions, I have gained a lot of experience in creating a unique value proposition and meeting my goals both professionally and personally. Patrick and I often laughed that every two years, it was a baby, then a promotion, a baby, then a promotion. I worked hard to gain varied experience and interact with my teams to understand the work and the people and what drives success in both. With each position from marketing to sales, customer experience and now president, I have found that having a positive attitude, believing in yourself and having a dream and a plan to get there are foundational. I believe these tips work not just for women but for anyone who aspires to professional achievement. I also recommend the following as part of anyone's playbook for success:

- **Seek out mentors.**
It's important to find and learn from men and women who you admire. Ask them to share their career playbook with you; the good ones will be absolutely enthusiastic about doing it.

- **Keep Learning.**
Knowledge is power, so always read and stay current on important topics to help you get ahead and stay relevant.

- **Set Goals.**
Write down your goals, personal and professional, then tell people about them. Visualize those goals and determine what small steps you can take toward each. It's difficult to hit a target if you don't even know what you are shooting at!

- **Don't be bashful.**
Let your career intentions be known, and by all means, have a voice at the table.

- **Let it go.**
When a door shuts, don't assume that it's the end. Expect and look for another door or opportunity that will open and let the closed door go.

- **Treat People Well.**
FedEx thrives on its PSP (people-service-profit) philosophy, and that applies to individuals as well. Treat your people well and with the utmost respect. They, in turn, will provide exceptional service to your customers, which will create profit for shareholders that can be reinvested back into the people. You must always treat people exactly how you would want to be treated and never forget that.

- **Choose gratitude.**
  I've always been an optimistic person, even when things did not go as I had hoped or planned. I am convinced of the power of our thoughts, and that we believe what we think. We should always choose the good thoughts even on the hard days.

- **Practice mindfulness and self-care.**
  It's critical you take care of you.

- **Make self-awareness and self-reflection daily habits.**
  It's a pivotal factor in whether you'll succeed.

- **Remember happiness is an inside job.**
  Happiness should never be dependent on a person, place or thing. It comes from within.

- **Surround yourself with people places and things that inspire you.**
  This will always help lift you up especially on the down days — which we all have.

- **Believe in yourself.**
  If you don't, how can you expect others to? Pay attention to your inner voice because we inevitably believe what we tell ourselves.

I close with one of the best lessons I have ever received. Just a year after Patrick's death, I received a phone call from FedEx headquarters in Memphis, Tenn., congratulating me on being chosen as the new president of FedEx Express in Canada. I was the first female and the first Canadian to hold the position. I was so surprised by the call and said, "Aren't you going to interview me?" The response was incredible: "You've been interviewing for 18 years." In any position, you are constantly interviewing. Live as if each 24-hour increment, each relationship, each project is an interview — giving your best to pursue this precious gift of life with grit, optimism and courage.

What details or lessons in this story resonate with me? And why?

How will I apply what I read or learned to my own career or personal life?

" A smooth sea never made a skilled sailor. "
- Franklin D. Roosevelt

Kawal

Preet

Regional President, Asia Pacific, Middle East and Africa
FedEx Express

Grit is a collection of choices that we make every day.

Grit is a collection of choices that we make every day. Most of us are used to hearing about what choices we should make. But sometimes it is more meaningful to look at choices that we should not make. Many women inadvertently set limits on themselves by choosing a mindset of self-doubt, choosing to stay in the background, and not taking risks or pursuing a dream because they lack courage and underestimate their abilities. Our mindsets arguably kill more dreams than failure ever does.

I grew up in Bhopal, India. For the most part, I had a normal middle-class upbringing. Both my parents worked, and our family values were around the idea that if you work hard, then you'll achieve. Their dedication to their professions has always been an inspiration to me. My dad is a civil engineer and worked in the construction industry. My mum has a master's degree in zoology and has worked all her life as a high school teacher.

When I was 10 years old, two pivotal events happened. The first was the assassination of our female Prime Minister Indira Gandhi by members of the Sikh community, followed by anti-Sikh riots across the country. I belong to the Sikh community, and Sikh men can be easily recognized with their turbans. I remember returning home from a 10-day school camp when chaos broke out. Many of the trains were cancelled. We didn't know what was going on, and we were all very fearful as we journeyed back home. When I arrived back, my dad wasn't there to meet me, which was an immediate shock. A colleague from his work arrived to take me home. There was limited movement in the city, and all the things we'd taken for granted quickly changed.

Because Sikhs were being targeted, we couldn't go out in town; we couldn't go shopping; we had to be quiet at home. More than 3,000 Sikhs died in those riots — a horrifying number. Despite the fear, when I pause and reflect, what stands out is the balanced attitude my family adopted, one more of hope than fear. A quiet courage, if you like. Our family was spared, but the mere threat of violence taught me about courage and compassion for others.

The second pivotal moment was the Bhopal gas tragedy — one of the world's worst industrial disasters. A huge gas leak from a pesticide plant had exposed more than half a million people to a toxic gas cloud. Thousands died in the immediate aftermath and from the effects of the gas in the years that followed. On the morning it happened, I was just a young girl going to school, waiting at the bus stop. But the bus never came, and the roads were unusually quiet. Rumors started flying. It's not like today where social media instantly tells you what's happening — we didn't yet know the extent of the chaos. All we knew was that our part of town didn't seem to be in the direct path of the gas cloud, so we stayed home — but no one really knew for sure. We had just moved to the new part of the town into a new house with some renovation work ongoing. A construction worker came by, panicked because his son was on the other side of the hill closer to the plant. He pleaded with my dad to help bring his son home. I remember family members saying to my dad, "It's a big gas leak — do you really think you should help?" But without hesitation, my dad simply grabbed a cloth to protect his face, jumped on a scooter, and helped bring that man's son safely home. This was the moment when my dad became my hero — and taught me about having real courage when you need it.

While the lessons I learned growing up in India may seem far removed from my leadership journey at FedEx, it strikes me that even though I was exposed to great courage early on, it took me much longer to learn how to have the courage to stop the self-doubt and the confidence to dream big. Growing up, I didn't dream big — I was actually quite contained in my vision for the future. I thought I'd go into the civil service. When I chose to study engineering, it never occurred to me that I was entering a field where women were a minority. In fact, it was only when I got to university — a co-ed college where I was just one of six girls in a class of 60 boys — that I learned to raise my hand and have a voice in order to be visible. That experience set the tone for what was to come.

My first job was at TATA Motors, one of the leading Indian multinationals, where I was just one of eight women among 300 men in engineering. There the men told me, "The girls who work here don't do nights because they need to be able to drive a pick-up truck if there's ever a problem." I had to say, "Hey, I can do that. I can drive a pick-up."

After I moved to Singapore, I wanted to work for a company that could take advantage of my electrical engineering skills. I interviewed at FedEx but didn't get the job. Luckily, I was called back for a second interview and was offered an associate engineer position where I was quickly exposed to a broader world — a world where I was actively encouraged to contribute my thoughts, opinions and ideas.

One of the big turning points in my career came early on when I was in a meeting listening to senior management debating the merits of a particular project. I chimed in with my view. Suddenly, everyone in the room stopped and looked at me. My first thought was, "Maybe I shouldn't have done that." I even said, "Sorry, should

I not have spoken?" But they said, "No, go on." They genuinely wanted to hear what I had to say. And that's the moment I found my voice. I fundamentally believe FedEx taught me how to dream.

We hear about disruption every day, but one of the first things that I've had to do every step of my own career is to disrupt my own thinking about myself and my capabilities. I've now had eight roles with FedEx. What's become clear along the way is that mindset is one of our biggest barriers to progress.

I am now facing yet another big disruption, and mindset will play a key role. My son, Harshul, just graduated high school and will be going to study at Carnegie Mellon College of Engineering, over 8,000 miles away. He is a really good kid, with a good head on his shoulders. I am proud that he still shares and communicates well with me, which is often a challenge with teenagers. He plays the oboe, and I have not missed a single school event so far. It's going to be very difficult to send him off to the U.S., but that's a new phase to which we both will have to adapt.

The rest of my family is all in India. I call my mum daily, usually on my way home from work. I also keep in touch with my extended family — uncles, aunties and cousins. These days, technology helps us stay connected, and I'm certain Harshul and I will use every app there is to continue to stay in touch when he is so far away.

Several years ago, I spoke to a large women's event with the theme "Nothing is Impossible." I told them what we perceive as "impossible" at any given point always needs to be re-examined, revisited and unpacked until we transform it into "I'm possible." How do you do that? I have relied on four principles to help me make confident choices throughout my career:

- **Recognize and eliminate a self-doubt mindset.**
We have all hesitated to go after a job, project, or personal challenge at some point because it wasn't the right time, and there are often very good reasons why people defer, avoid or procrastinate over these decisions. But my experience has been that there are always equally good reasons why it's sometimes best to just go for it. When an opportunity or choice presents itself, we must learn to unpack all the reasons behind the options we are considering — or find a trusted advisor to help. Are we inadvertently holding ourselves back? Are we unconsciously setting our own glass ceiling through our choices or lack of choices? I have been fortunate at every stage of my FedEx career to have great mentors who have pushed me to challenge myself and to stop underestimating my abilities.

Mindset as a factor in our success is a well-documented field. For instance, Stanford University professor of psychology Carol Dweck's work on "growth" versus "fixed" mindset is considered ground-breaking. She believes that much of what might prevent us from fulfilling our potential grows out of mindset. In a fixed mindset, you believe your basic abilities are immovable — you have a certain amount and that's it — whereas when you're in more of a growth mindset, you believe those abilities, those talents, even your intelligence can be developed through hard work, good strategies and lots of help and input from others. And if so, how can we unlearn certain skills so that even if the train comes off the tracks, we can take our success to the next level?

- **Don't put a limit on your dreams.**
We all have different experiences and traditions which shape our lives. When I was a single working woman in India, at just 22 years of age, my parents decided it was time for me to get married. So, in line with my cultural tradition, I had an arranged marriage. I didn't really question it, because it was just what you did back then. Although that marriage took me to Singapore, where I joined FedEx, and brought me my beautiful son, the relationship didn't last. Suffice it to say, it was tough. I felt a lot of guilt, and I couldn't understand why I'd been successful at so much but not at this.

Of course, it was exactly at this moment that one of my biggest career opportunities thus far decided to present itself — a managing director role in Planning & Engineering in Hong Kong. My initial thoughts were, "My marriage had just ended, my son is so young, is it the right time?" I was encouraged to talk to the hiring manager. Even my grandfather wisely said to me, "Why are you putting a limit on your dreams just because you're a mother?" And he was right.

I decided to put my hand up and interview for the job — and I got it. Making the very difficult decision to end my marriage, moving from Singapore to Hong Kong with a two-year-old in tow to take on a very challenging role, and raising my son on my own with no nearby family or friend support was not easy; it took a lot of grit. I could not have done it without the folks at FedEx, who were the village supporting me on the journey. There have been days that I just wanted to give up, but my faith and my son keep me going. So, as the saying goes, "Pain is inevitable; suffering is optional." I think we all have times of difficulty, even crisis, when the path forward feels like a risk that is too great. Yet, in so many situations in my life, what I thought was impossible was, in fact, possible.

- **Keep Learning. Stretch!**
Whatever your capabilities, learn to stretch them to the limit and a little beyond. Take risks and be open to uncertainty. Because that is when the momentum often comes and when the personal and career growth happens. At a time when disruption is everywhere, developing a mindset that is open to thinking ahead, embracing complexity and harnessing change has never been more important. I'm grateful to those who have pushed me along, given me a nudge or even a genuine jolt. We all have to be willing to deal with a certain amount of discomfort in order to see what we're truly capable of, and I would encourage you, at every possible moment, to be intentional about seeking out challenging work. In many ways, this is about stepping beyond the confines of our comfort zones and expanding our confidence to stretch both personally and professionally. Try new things — and do not be afraid — even when something is intimidating.

- **Walk Tall**
A particularly strong female boss in Hong Kong saw in me what I didn't see in myself and generously mentored me. She told me I needed to "walk tall." And I thought, "But what does that mean?" — especially since I am usually the shortest person in any room. She also said I should "sit at the table." Again, I would ask, "But what exactly does that mean?" I didn't completely understand it at the time, but she was coaching me to master executive presence — a presence that I didn't yet have. She made it a point to include me in meetings with vocal peers. She'd fire

questions at me. She said, "Let's have Kawal answer this." It often made me uncomfortable — sometimes even upset me — but by doing that, she purposefully put me in situations which pushed me to be better than my excuses and bigger than my fears.

Even now, I need to constantly challenge myself and cultivate a growth mindset. For instance, when a senior vice president role came up — an extraordinary opportunity — my first thought was, "There are others more experienced than me. I will give it my best, and it's okay if I don't get it." When I shared my thoughts with a colleague, he looked me straight in the eye, challenged me and gave me a jolt. It changed my trajectory, personally and in my career.

I also recommend taking time to relax. I take evening walks when I don't have night calls with the U.S. I love listening to Bollywood music and podcasts, and I love to read to relax and rejuvenate. I also practice mindfulness and meditation to maintain inner peace. This is especially important considering the dynamic and chaotic external environment in which we live and over which we have so little control.

Today, my role as president of the Asia Pacific, Middle East and Africa Region of FedEx Express continues to present opportunities for me to step out of my comfort zone, take risks and pursue dreams that others may think impossible. I'm responsible for the combined air and ground operations of FedEx in more than 103 markets, with 40,000 team members. It's a big job, and a long way from my roots growing up in India. But those lessons in focusing on a positive and confident mindset, standing tall and allowing my voice to be heard, have and continue to be the right choices. I continue to navigate through a lot of storms that I cannot control, but I know with confidence that adjusting my sails is a choice I can control. I urge all women to do the same. Make the choice to believe in yourself. Quash that self-doubt. As the saying goes, "When you can't change the direction of the wind, adjust your sails" and dream big!

What details or lessons in this story resonate with me? And why?

How will I apply what I read or learned to my own career or personal life?

> *"We will forever be known by the tracks we leave behind us."*
> *- Native American Dakota Tribe*

Bobbi Wells

Vice President,
Safety and Airworthiness
FedEx Express

I grew up the second of four siblings in a very small town in the mountains of Wyoming. We were all very active in competitive and recreational sports as well as music. My dad was an outdoorsman who taught us to be resilient and to persevere. He encouraged us to attempt new things and if we chose something to try, we worked at it until we could do it well. He was someone we didn't want to disappoint. One of his favorite sayings was tied to snow skiing, but he insisted we apply it to everything we did: "If you're not falling down, you're not learning."

My mom taught me to be independent. She ran her own business for over 50 years while raising four kids. She is fiercely loyal and has always encouraged us, no matter the challenge. She is one of the grittiest people I know — the kind of person who takes care of things during difficult times rather than simply sitting back and worrying about them. She's also very brave and adventurous. She learned to scuba dive because she knew my dad had a passion for it. They took diving trips all over the world.

Dad never once told me I couldn't do something because I was a girl, so it never occurred to me that my gender might limit my opportunities. I found out otherwise when I joined the Army. While stationed in Germany, a commander told me he did not give me a command position because, as he said, "I'm giving the job to Dan. He works because he has to. You work because you want to." When things like this happen, I hear Dad's voice telling me to push on. Another of his favorite expressions: "When someone thinks you can't do something, it's their problem, not yours."

During my time in the Army, I had many opportunities to develop grit and test my endurance. There were physical and mental challenges that

> Grit is the will to persevere in the face of difficulties — small, medium, or huge. It is the desire to follow through even if the challenge you may be facing seems overwhelming. It's hanging tough because giving up isn't an alternative.

pushed me farther than I thought I would ever be able to go. There were times when the environment wasn't supportive of women. I reported to my first unit at Fort Sill, Oklahoma, when I was six months pregnant. That was at a time when the Army was not supportive of pregnant service members. My company commander told me he couldn't believe I would show up at my first duty station pregnant. If we had to go to war, I was undeployable, and he saw that as shirking my duty and damaging my leadership credibility. I told him that as difficult as my pregnancy might be on my soldiers, sergeants and him, it was much harder on me. Once I delivered the baby, I knew it would be critical for me to get back into shape so I could go through physical training with my soldiers. I worked hard to get back up to speed, and I knew my commander was proud of my ability to bounce back. It was not easy, but by pushing every day and believing in myself, I did it.

The biggest personal triumph from my time in the Army came when I had opportunities to face and overcome longstanding fears. I was frequently placed in situations of significant responsibility for missions for which I had little or no experience. I encountered physical challenges, such as a 10K midnight run through the woods in Germany in combat gear and with a full pack and weapon. While I may not have finished in first place in those tests, simply completing the challenges felt like a triumph. At the same time, it reinforced the importance of growth through the journey. I felt satisfaction in knowing that I could endure and accomplish things I never imagined I could, in an environment that was often less than hospitable.

Be open to possibilities rather than viewing your future as a narrow, well-defined path.

I didn't know where my Army service would lead me or what opportunities would follow. So, throughout my life, I have tried to be open to possibilities rather than viewing my future as a narrow, well-defined path. That has allowed me to do jobs and take career and personal paths I never envisioned. I have learned that being confident in your ability to make a difference will put you on a path to realize your dreams. It may not happen on the precise route or timeline you expect, but with tenacity and focus, you can achieve what you desire.

During my last year of service, I was assigned to FedEx as part of the "Training with Industry" program. I found the culture, mission and values of FedEx to be aligned with what was important to me and knew I could find a home at FedEx. I was right!

Just three months into my first position at FedEx, the confidence and leadership I learned in the Army came into play. I was senior manager of the downtown station in New York City when the World Trade Center was attacked with a car bomb. I had a courier in my station whom my managers had warned me was "trouble." Being new to FedEx, I wasn't sure what "trouble" looked like compared to what I'd experienced with Army soldiers, so I started keeping an eye on this employee.

Then, the day of the car-bombing, he came in to start his pickup route. There was a great deal of chaos in the city and at our station that day. But as usual, the courier signed for his equipment, picked up his supplies and headed out to start his route, which included the World Trade Center. When he arrived there, he talked his way past the barricades because he knew the police. He talked his way into the loading dock because he knew the building security guards. He proceeded to retrieve every single customer package and brought them back to the station where they went into the system for delivery the next day. I discovered that the managers considered him "trouble" because he sometimes asked difficult questions in workgroup meetings. He also pushed back — respectfully — when he didn't think an answer made sense. The truth was that he made the managers feel uncomfortable. He was smart, analytical and a problem solver. Obviously, he was also dedicated and tough. He cared about his customers. On that challenging day, he did more than I would have ever asked him to do. I awarded him a Bravo Zulu, a military term adopted by FedEx to reward a job well done.

At FedEx, there are plenty of situations that demand steady and resolute leadership during crisis. I faced one of the most challenging in the aftermath of the terrorist attacks on 9/11. I was a senior manager in Global Operations Control where we had responsibility to manage all FedEx aircraft worldwide. Bringing the FedEx airline back up after that crisis was not easy logistically, not only because of the unique security requirements that had grounded the planes, but also because of the emotional impact on each of our team members. Most recently, during the COVID-19 pandemic, I led a coordination contingency team for 10,000 FedEx Air Operations employees. In this situation, we had to keep things going and remain productive while protecting pilots and ground safety maintenance teams with masks and sanitation procedures.

My advice to women today is never stop that learning process and approach any challenge with confidence, courage and boldness.

As my career continues to grow, I am still "falling down and learning." I think my dad would be proud. My advice to women today is to never stop that learning process and approach any challenge with confidence, courage and boldness. If I could impart advice based on my journey, I would focus on six things:

Team Matters
Throughout my military and FedEx careers, I have learned that surrounding yourself with a strong team is critical. Success doesn't come from going it alone. Mentors have been an important part of my professional life — people next to and above me who have coached me through challenges and influenced and inspired through their own example. I have known some of them for many years and treasure our relationships. I work to be the same kind of leader as they have been for me. I never take for granted that I have a unique opportunity to influence and inspire people every day as a leader in aviation and officer in one of the world's top companies. The desire to make a difference to people individually and through a great

collaborative working environment is a role I don't take lightly. I am intentional about creating impact by working on my communications skills, assessing and adjusting my style, and ensuring people know that I sincerely care about them and their success. The best leaders in history see beyond the horizon and behave with integrity. The best leaders truly care for people. My dad always told me everyone deserves kindness and it never goes out of style.

The best leaders in history see beyond the horizon and behave with integrity.

- **Team applies personally as well!**
I have been fortunate to have had a supportive husband, Mark, and sons — Chris and Markus — who are comfortable around strong women. Both of my sons now work in aviation, so we have chances to share our common interests. I learn from them and Kristelle, my daughter-in-law, who is also in aviation, every time we talk. My husband is not only my best friend, he is my biggest cheerleader and the one who guides me most. He has also always been the one to sacrifice, though he would never look at it that way. He is generously flexible if I want to do something. He found his own success working security for the U.S. Treasury Department despite having to move every time the Army or FedEx reassigned me. He is incredibly smart, a dedicated dad and the rock in our family.

- **Be intentional about balance and trade-offs in every decision.**
People sometimes ask if I have missed things in life in exchange for success in my career. Mark and I chose to live a life that took us far from our families, which meant fewer holidays and birthdays with everyone. However, when we do visit, our time together is all the sweeter. Along with work and family, I have many hobbies: I dive, water ski, snow ski, play the piano, flute, and trombone, and am also a voracious reader. I have developed a reading list I happily share with leaders inside and outside of FedEx. Two great books on my desk right now are "Grit: The Power of Passion and Perseverance" by Angela Lee Duckworth, and "Power of Purpose" by Richard Lieder.

- **Be all you can be.**
My favorite Army slogan, "Be all you can be," is one I have lived by. There have been times when I have been treated differently because I am a woman, but I do not worry about anyone discounting my input when I'm the only woman in the room. I honestly doubt if they are considering that as they respond. If I am wrong, I have lost nothing by being myself and contributing what I believe will make the organization better. I am not responsible for their opinion about whether I belong or not. I am only responsible for providing a good example. And my message for women — whether you are being discriminated against or not — is to believe in yourself. Go for the impossible because it can become your possible.

Don't walk by a mistake.

I have learned that nothing is ever as hard as it seems, and nothing is as easy as you might like. There are no shortcuts, and no one is going to swoop in and save you. Be prepared and believe you can do it; don't walk away from problems when things are not easy. I am tenacious and willing to do hard things. My first Army company commander and I were talking about the requirements of leaders. He explained that the privilege of leadership comes with an obligation. Leaders don't walk past a mistake. If you do, you endorse it. As human beings, we prefer avoiding controversy that happens when we challenge someone or try to change a process. But our responsibility as a leader doesn't just apply when it's convenient. "Don't walk by a mistake" has become one of our FedEx safety mantras.

Be Brave.

I do not want to look back on my life and be sorry for things I didn't have the courage to do. Courage is not a single act. It comes from being brave in small bits that add up to a courageous approach to life. We can all be brave for 20 seconds at a time, and that's all it usually takes to overcome what frightens us. And if we fail or make a mistake? We simply learn, let it go and grow. We "fall down, get back up and keep learning."

I am honored to be the first woman to hold my position in aviation at FedEx. But that is only one reason I am so happy to go to work each morning. Every day, I am inspired by my team. It is a pure pleasure for me to see the faces of team members light up when a daily mission is accomplished.

Bravo Zulu indeed!

What details or lessons in this story resonate with me? And why?

How will I apply what I read or learned to my own career or personal life?

> *"You may not control all the events that happen to you, but you can decide not to be reduced by them."*
> *- Dr. Maya Angelou*

Gloria

Roberts Boyland

Retired
Corporate Vice President,
Operations and Service Support
FedEx Corporation

True grit is having the strength of character to persevere through a challenge, to dig down and find what is necessary to overcome. Do I have it? Yes! In fact, I believe every single one of us has grit, but so often we don't use it. Grit is a deliberate choice made in small and large decisions.

I am a daughter of the South, born and raised in Georgia. My childhood was filled with joy, curiosity, the beauty of art and the love of family. I credit my mom as my best and earliest mentor. She taught me about the world and broadened my horizons through art and reading. During visits to museums, she showed me that works of art are more than physical sculptures or paintings. Beyond the surface, they can become windows to new thoughts and places. I was a girl who sought library books and soaked in history to travel intellectually.

My grandmother opened my eyes to the need in our world and inspired me to work hard and believe in myself. She told me that education matters. Not giving up on a dream matters. She encouraged me to overcome stereotypes by doing and showing everyone who I really am. My grandmother told me, "Gloria, there will be times when others will undervalue you because you are Black and female, but you need to find ways to rise above the situation." She taught me to never see myself as a victim, and to remind myself that I am vibrant, smart and capable even when others may say the opposite. She taught me to ignore the doubters, rely on family, friends and most importantly, your own strength and grit.

If my family gave me roots and wings, my friends provided jet fuel and ballast. I am so fortunate to have close friends who live across the U.S. and around the globe. Through the various phases of my life, my friends and colleagues have served as kind provocateurs, demanding teachers and

> True grit is having the strength of character to persevere through a challenge, to dig down and find what is necessary to overcome.

inspiring gurus. The most enduring mentor relationships I have had are with my close circle of friends whose objectives were aligned with mine, but who were still willing to be honest and provide a different perspective. They helped challenge me to identify strengths and never settle for anything less than my best.

My natural curiosity, love of reading and desire to have all the facts contributed to my initial career choice as an attorney. Law provided an intellectual challenge and an opportunity to build on my love of words and right brain creativity. However, a few years into my legal career, I transitioned to a different kind of storytelling, one through data. I became a commercial transactions attorney where I developed an appreciation for numbers-based logic. I discovered that I could excel when I combined both types of thinking to build a strong case. I spent 12 years at General Electric Co. in mergers-and-acquisitions which gave me an opportunity to work across myriad business models and varied cultures. I traveled the world and worked closely with so many diverse teams. As a leader, it became a revelation to me to see how much commonality exists within such apparently wide diversity.

My life journey has taken me far from my southern roots and now back again. An airport bus driver once told me that he considered me to be brave because I ventured so far from home to build a life. I explained to him that I really didn't feel brave at all. I had nothing to fear because I have always had reinforcements readily available anytime I went some place new.

The hardest things in life can often be our greatest teachers.

Often, the hardest things in life can be our greatest teachers. During my last four years at GE, I received valuable on-the-job training in the politics of power. In that difficult position, I learned firsthand that not everyone has integrity. I learned the hard way that some people will never see you as you are because of their focus on elevating themselves or, in some cases, long-held stereotypes. That experience gave me the drive to seek out a new opportunity, to not settle for a less than desirable work environment.

It took a year of searching for just the right position, but I found an incredible new job and company in a vice president position at FedEx. The position offered advancement, a new adventure and a chance to lead strong teams in making a difference globally. My career at FedEx has allowed me to go beyond my early days of "virtual travel" through books and museums to see the world, experience the culture and get to know people from other countries. So far, I have ventured to 40 countries. Traveling has given me firsthand insight that despite diverse backgrounds, ethnicities, genders or race, community does exist through the common core of humanity that runs through all of us. We just need to take the time to look.

I am now retired from my position as corporate vice president of Operations and Service Support at FedEx. I was not actively looking for this position when the opportunity arose. The candidate field was exceptionally strong, but timing and encouragement from mentors led me to go for it with confidence and get the job. In this position, I expanded into innovation and advanced operations technologies, which was very exciting. I am especially proud of my role in developing FedEx's Quality Driven Management system and revamping the Service Quality Index which measures critical experience touchpoints that drive customer loyalty. For that work, I received one of our company's highest honors, the Five Star Award. And just as important, I was given a sense of personal achievement that my team and I had made a difference for the company.

Appreciate the strength of friends and family and make the most out of the life we have been given.

My most terrifying life challenge was breast cancer. Despite the pain and uncertainty with chemotherapy, surgery and recovery, I have learned some valuable lessons from my fight with cancer. I learned the importance of letting go, and appreciated the strength of friends and family. I am making the most out of the life I have been given.

Reflecting on my experiences, I would give other women seven principles to navigate life successfully:

- **Be prepared.**
Whether a new job, a new place to live, a decision to be made, always be prepared for new opportunities so that what you bring to the table is the best you have to offer.

- **Build a tribe.**
Throughout my life, my network of family, friends and coworkers have encouraged, motivated and provided different perspectives. I have experienced joy, security, accomplishment, financial success, discrimination, personal loss and breast cancer. But I wasn't alone. Build your network, rely on family and friends — a tribe that will make you stronger in all areas of life.

- **Never stop learning.**
I have always sought knowledge through art, travel, mentoring and sharing. Learning and growing should be a lifelong goal. Working with Fred Smith at FedEx was always filled with learning moments, gaining knowledge from him and others in the company that empowered, challenged and made me a better person and leader. He expected excellence and always urged us to give our best. Working with him was like attending the best business leadership program in the world.

- **Earn loyalty.**
I often share that loyalty is earned. Earned by doing the right thing, by increasing your company's value to the customer, by being there for others, by being a friend. Loyalty is worth earning.

- **Give Back.**
As a cancer survivor, I knew the value of support — from friends and family to doctors and nurses. Today, I give back as a way of showing my gratitude for the care I received. I sit on two corporate boards, am a community action partner and a cancer survivor/thriver. I am building an entrepreneurial venture, Butterfly LLC, to provide better post-surgical options for breast cancer survivors/thrivers. Because I am grateful to be a breast cancer survivor myself, profits from that company will be redeployed to support others fighting cancer.

- **Be humble.**
It takes bravery to always be accountable for one's actions and the impact they have on others. I have had to say, "I am sorry," and, "That was my fault," many times in life. Be a leader who succeeds but also one who humbly admits when mistakes are made.

- **Be tough.**
Be clear on what is important to you and the value you bring. Confidently raise your hand — and voice if necessary — when you have something to say and ask for opportunities. Listen to others and seek input, but be insistent on being heard on behalf of what you know is right for you, your company and the people in it.

I live my life today as I did when I was growing up as a child visiting museums and reading books: with a sense of wonder and curiosity. Most importantly, I live my life with gratitude, welcoming opportunities to give back and share just as others did for me.

What details or lessons in this story resonate with me? And why?

How will I apply what I read or learned to my own career or personal life?

Tracci Schultz

Senior Vice President, Strategic Planning, Engineering and Operational Solutions
FedEx Freight

> True grit is in all of us; we just need the strength to tap into the courage, determination and perseverance it takes to succeed.

" Leadership is not about titles, positions or flow charts. It is about one life influencing another. "
- John C. Maxwell

You may have heard people say that they "grew up" at FedEx. For me, it's true. I joined the company when I was 19 years old and would never have imagined that I would still be here today reflecting on a 35-year career — and counting.

I was raised in a small town where everyone knew everyone. My parents were high school sweethearts who got married before graduating. They had three children. I am the middle child with an older brother and younger sister. My dad was a baseball and football coach and my mother was the CEO of our home. They did their best to provide for us while balancing work and family. Growing up, our lives revolved around sports which gave us a large community of friends with whom we spent time at ball fields, on vacations and on weekend camping trips. That is where I learned how to connect with people and to be independent.

I was also blessed to have the best grandparents a child could ask for. My mother's parents lived in the country while my father's mother lived in the city. I got the best of both worlds by spending time in the summer with all my grandparents. In the country, I could run free in the cotton field while learning about the demands of farming. Then, I would visit my other grandmother who ran her own company and taught me the challenges of business.

I grew up with the love, support and encouragement of three strong, courageous and inspiring women. They shaped me into the person I am today. My mother ran a tight ship, kept a perfectly manicured yard, a pristine house and provided a home-cooked meal on the table every night. My grandmother who lived in the country took on a job in Memphis to supplement her income. She commuted 90 minutes to work and balanced the demands of a full-time job in a physician's office with the requirements of running a farm. My other grandmother was a widow with the tremendous responsibility of running her own business. All three demonstrated unwavering courage every day without a thought of giving up. I recall so many times when I would be with my grandmothers after a long day at work and, as tired and stressed as they likely were, they still gave me their undivided attention, listening to all my seemingly huge issues and problems. My mother helped me raise my kids after working long hours herself. And as my own family grew, all three of those strong women invested so much of their time and energy in me, my siblings and my children, shaping our lives in so many positive ways. When someone asks me to define true grit, I merely point to those three ladies. They embodied the meaning of grit!

Even the launch of my career is linked to my mother in a humorous twist. When I graduated from high school, I received a credit card offer in the mail from a local department store. I had longed for an Aigner purse, so I decided to sign up for the card and use it to purchase the $140 purse. I was so excited to have it and carried it with great pride. Then, 30 days later, the bill arrived. My mother looked me in the eye and told me, "Sister, you better get yourself a job. I'm not paying that bill."

I don't know what I was expecting, but I realized then that I had to find a job and quickly. I signed up with a temporary agency and was assigned to FedEx as an interim receptionist. After a couple of months, I was offered a full-time position. I explained that I planned to go to college and was informed that FedEx would provide tuition reimbursement. I was thrilled because I wasn't sure how I was going to afford college.

In that first job with FedEx, my role was assistant to the assistant of a vice president. Yes, the assistant to the assistant. After two years, the Air Operations Information Services Director selected me as his administrative assistant, exposing me to a new leadership style and providing tremendous growth opportunities. I had a very encouraging leader who supported me in my college classes while giving me opportunities to take on assignments beyond the normal role of an assistant. That led to a promotion into a coordinator role where I could learn from leaders across the company.

Like many working women, I quickly learned the value of a support system. We can't do it all alone! I often felt guilty about work and family trade-offs: choosing between meetings and school functions or caring for a sick child while trying to manage work issues. Flying off on a business trip while missing school events or even passing up career advancement opportunities to support family needs. Yes, there were days I felt like a failure on all fronts. But my husband, Mark, was my anchor and biggest supporter. I remember him going to work early so that he could get off in time to make it to the day care and avoid the ten-dollar-per-minute late fee. When I was balancing college, career and family, he took on even more responsibilities at home so I could focus on my schoolwork. When I was nervous about presentations or project issues, he was my tireless sounding board and provided inspiring pep talks. And when I needed to travel abroad and was uneasy about flying from Memphis to China by myself, he encouraged me and eased my nerves. But the most impactful and important thing he has done is to voluntarily allow his own ambitious career goals to take a backseat to mine.

I completed my undergraduate degree after attending college for seven years, while juggling roles of wife, mother and full-time employee. Yes, I felt overwhelmed at times. It took determination and perseverance — sometimes more of both traits than I thought I had. There were moments when I felt the trade-offs that I had to make were unfair to one area or the other. But I knew that to be successful at each, I needed to stay focused and do my best. In the end, I graduated with honors, proving the importance of structure, goals and perseverance to my young daughter, and to myself. I can proudly say that I am the first female in my family to complete college and the only female so far to earn a master's degree.

As I advanced with the company, we decided it would be better if my husband resigned from his job to be present in the daily lives of our kids. This was a bold move for him. He had been an all-star athlete in high school and college. He was an award-winning sales professional. He was in a leadership position at his company. And, quite frankly, at that time, neither of us knew of anyone who had reversed traditional roles like we were about to do.

We made a conscious decision that our family would be part of a journey that would show our children the value of non-traditional working parents, loving partnerships and persevering through life's adversities. I am proud of our family and particularly our children — Amanda, Dalton and Dillon — because we have truly been on this journey together, and the sacrifices we've made collectively have allowed us to create a meaningful legacy.

A pivotal moment in my career and family life came through an exciting promotion — CIO/vice president of FedEx Office. The position required relocating to Dallas, the first time we would live away from our extended family. It would inevitably disrupt the lives of our kids. But it was a wonderful opportunity, as I would be able to see all aspects of running a company, which is highly unusual for an IT officer. The family sat down around the kitchen table and discussed it at length. Our daughter was married by then, and she could not imagine that we would move away and leave her behind. Our boys, who were about to be a junior and a senior in high school, were, to our surprise, all in on the idea and thrilled by the opportunity.

However, when I accepted the position and we relocated to Dallas, the boys' lives were turned upside-down and inside-out. They had not fully realized what it would be like to leave behind their lifelong friends, family members, their school, their baseball teams and more. Before long, they were begging to be allowed to move back to Memphis and live with their sister. We decided to let our oldest son move back and complete his senior year and are so grateful to our daughter for going along with the plan. We also decided it would be best to have our younger son remain with us and complete high school in Dallas. I will not deny that this proved to be a very challenging two years that brought the grit out in all of us.

As I was wrapping up my second year in Dallas, we learned that our daughter was expecting our first grandchild. That made us even more eager to return to Memphis. As luck would have it, one of my peers was planning his retirement, and I was offered the position. Right place at the right time? Perhaps, but luck is when opportunity meets preparation, so you should always be prepared for the next opportunity.

They don't always arrive on your timeline like this one did, but preparation along with perseverance is a powerful combination. This new role was such a blessing for me and my family. It allowed us to return to Memphis and reunite our family.

The opportunities are limitless at FedEx, but they don't always come knocking. I encourage women in any stage of your career to seek opportunity or create it yourself. Don't hold yourself back by focusing on what you don't have. Instead, double down on your strengths and surround yourself with people and knowledge to learn and find new opportunities for growth. I am proof that it works. I have worked in 12 different departments and held 15 different positions across the company. I've worked for 21 great bosses who taught me so much over the years. I've worked in and/or supported FedEx Express, FedEx Office, FedEx Freight and FedEx Services which exposed me to the inner workings of FedEx as well as what our customers expect of us. If I can do it, you can, too.

> **Preparation along with perseverance is a powerful combination.**

One thing that stands out over my 35 years with the company is the gratitude for my FedEx family. The love and support extended by my peers, my mentors and my leaders through all of life's milestones, expected and unexpected, made a difference. I got married, had three children, had multiple medical procedures and lost loved ones. FedEx has been there every step of the way. My vice president attended my wedding. That was a shock to many in my family who had worked for big companies for years and had never even seen a vice president in person. When my kids were born, my peers were at the hospital and sent food for my family throughout my maternity leave. When my grandmother passed away, my director drove two hours to attend the visitation. When my mother passed away, my team showered me with love and support because they knew just how much she meant to me and my family. Through baby showers, weddings and visitation services, I have always been surrounded by the love and support of my FedEx family.

> **Double down on your strengths and surround yourself with people and knowledge to learn and find new opportunities for growth.**

I hope you see yourself somewhere in my story. And I hope you embrace what it takes to succeed just as my parents and grandparents taught me early on.

True grit is in all of us; we just need the strength to tap into the courage, determination and perseverance it takes to succeed:

- **Courage.**
Courage to embrace the unknown, speak the truth, blaze the trails, adapt through coaching — especially when doing so is not the easiest route to take.

- **Determination.**
Determination to do what others may think to be impossible.

- **Perseverance.**
Perseverance to overcome adversity, the ability to apply lessons learned from both successes and failures and the strength to never allow fear to overcome outcomes.

Be confident in who you are as a person and be your best self. Self-doubt is a terrible thing, and the sooner you can put an end to it, the happier, healthier and more successful you will be. In all honesty, building your confidence is a lifetime journey. It certainly has been for me.

Today, I am still just as committed to doing my best as I was when I joined FedEx all those years ago. I am grateful for the journey and proud to be among and supported by a powerful group of women leaders who not only have true grit, but who have helped shape the culture of our great company and pave the way for the female leaders of tomorrow.

What details or lessons in this story resonate with me? And why?

How will I apply what I read or learned to my own career or personal life?

Cheryl
Pitzer

MD 11 Fleet Captain
FedEx Express Flight Operations

True grit comes from the perseverance to believe in yourself and the sustained fortitude to overcome obstacles.

" Do to others as you would have them do to you. "
- Luke 6:31

I suppose you could say I found my perfect career because I have always loved to travel. My grandfather used to tell me that I "was born with the wanderlust." As a pilot with FedEx, you can certainly say I have fulfilled that yearning to go places even though I have had my share of turbulence along the way.

I grew up in Arizona, and my family always traveled during summer vacation, which sparked my passion to see the world. We had a travel trailer and made our way to most of the U.S. I remember camping in Yellowstone National Park and visiting Bryce Canyon National Park and Zion National Park. During those summer trips, we saw the beauty and majesty of our country. We saw the history of our nation when we followed memorials and sites from the south all the way to Washington, D.C., Boston and Philadelphia.

Both of my parents worked at a time when mothers working outside the home was still uncommon. My mom was often criticized for working but her example taught me that I could grow up to be anything I wanted. She assured me that pursuing a career while having a family was possible. She convinced me that the sky was the limit.

I worked my way through college selling spring break trips to students. For every 10 trips I sold, I got to go on the trip for free which fed my love of traveling. Upon graduation, armed with a degree in advertising, I wanted to keep traveling, so I became a flight attendant while I looked for that perfect advertising job. One day, I stuck my head into the cockpit and saw the pilots in action. The view from the front of the aircraft hit me like a lightning bolt. That moment was pivotal — I knew that I wanted to fly.

I continued working as a flight attendant while taking flying lessons at Hooks Airport in Spring, Texas. Eventually, I got enough hours and obtained my ratings. Along the way I met Marcela, one of the few female managers of a charter company in the U.S. With the lack of female pilots in the industry, she not only became a good friend, but also a mentor with great advice. She warned me that being a female pilot would not be easy. She set a very high standard for conduct — advising me to stay focused, work hard, keep my nose clean and stick to my principles. Marcela reminded me that I would be a minority in a world of men so I had best develop thick skin. She also urged me to believe in myself and to not let anyone tell me I can't do something.

I took her advice to heart and built a successful flying career. There have been times in my career when I had to rely heavily on true grit to get through. I worked four jobs at the same time to build my flight hours and gain experience without taking a single day off. The path to becoming an airline pilot is long and difficult at times — especially as a female. Even today, approximately 92 percent of airline pilots in the U.S. are men. Early on, before joining FedEx, I experienced sexual harassment at the time when standing up for yourself did not feel like an option. If you did, you were labeled a troublemaker. It is still not easy, but over time enough women have bravely stood up to injustice so that we are now able to be heard and respected.

One of my first jobs was with a small carrier that contracted with FedEx. I got to know the FedEx crews and vowed to work for the company one day. It was not easy to get on with a prestigious organization like FedEx, but with patience and determination I eventually got my chance.

I have been with FedEx for 24 years now. Although most of our flights are smooth and uneventful, some require extra calm and grit in the face of the unexpected. One of my most memorable flights was on September 11, 2001. When the planes hit New York City's twin towers, my crew and I were flying from Hong Kong to Anchorage, Alaska. We were making our way along the coast of Asia, just about to head across the Pacific Ocean, when we got a message telling us the World Trade Center in New York City had been hit by a plane. Like most, we assumed it was an accident, then got the word that it was much worse and that it would impact us and most other aircraft in the sky at the time. Our crew exhibited the type of performance we at FedEx expect: we remained calm as we put a plan together. Since the closest airport to us was Tokyo, we contacted the tower there, only to learn they had just closed to incoming aircraft. We were able to convince them to allow us and several others to land. With all the worldwide confusion and with our incompatible cell phones, it took five days to put things back together and get us home.

After flying professionally for so many years, it is inevitable that you will encounter emergency situations. Pilots study aircraft accidents regularly and learn from them. The best pilots keep calm and rely on their own experience and company training. That is precisely what my crew did when we experienced a complete electrical failure while taking off from John F. Kennedy International Airport in New York. I was the Captain of the MD-11 and had never seen this type of problem. All our instruments were unreadable, and we were having severe problems with the flight controls, aileron, rudder and other basic tools we needed to be able to circle around and land the aircraft. Most disturbing of all — there was no checklist for proceeding. Up until that point, this type of failure was simply not possible. Despite the urgency of the situation, we instinctively knew that we would need to remain calm. Together we ultimately landed the aircraft safely, later receiving the CEO Safety Award for our actions. It is one of the highest awards given by FedEx. But in accepting the recognition, I gave my first officer and the air traffic control team the credit for their calm problem-solving. Without their input, skill and demeanor, the situation could have ended very differently.

A successful career is rarely a solo accomplishment – we all need help from others through mentoring, encouragement and support.

A successful career is rarely a solo accomplishment — we all need help from others through mentoring, encouragement and support. My husband Pete has always been supportive of every career choice I have made. I have had several jobs that are not typical for a pilot, including simulator and aircraft instructor/evaluator, FAA representative and now management pilot. These roles have sometimes meant being away from home more often than if I had been just flying a regular schedule. But Pete understands. Of course, marrying a fellow FedEx pilot helps make home life much easier. We both understand the unique challenges of balancing flying with being at home. We have each missed many holidays and special occasions. By marrying Pete, I also picked up an "instant" family since he had kids from a previous marriage. Those children are now married and have children of their own. Being a grandmother is so much fun!

Pete and I are committed to giving back. We met flying at FedEx and flew together on a flight to Ghana, Africa, to support Project Orbis, an actual eye hospital that just happens to operate from an airplane. This program began 30 years ago and has evolved to a state-of-the-art MD-10 donated by FedEx. The front of the aircraft has a 46-seat classroom where local doctors from developing nations can come to observe and learn vision-saving techniques from experienced doctors who operate in the sterile surgical unit in the rear of the aircraft. Project Orbis is a teaching hospital, and the aircraft has no "home." It constantly moves around the world, giving so many the gift of sight. The Orbis staff and volunteers are from all over the globe, coming together for the common goal of helping the world to see. The work the Orbis volunteers and staff do is life changing, and it is humbling for me to be a part of it. I have also been honored to fly on FedEx charitable missions following natural disasters.

Pete and I have similar goals when it comes to making the best out of life. Our life together began and continues as a big adventure: we were married in Australia and have continued to travel the world together ever since. One of the most interesting trips was to the island of Cypress, and then to Greece. Planes are not our only mode of transportation. Pete and I love to sail and even participated in several regattas. We particularly enjoy seeing and experiencing wildlife on our trips, including two

African safaris. To this day, my favorite FedEx flights are when we get to transport animals, especially the zoo and aquarium animals. That is the main reason Pete and I now own Lazy Dog Ranch in Nevada, Texas. Not only do we have horses and donkeys, but camels and one of my favorite pets, a "zdonkey," which is a cross between a zebra and a donkey. We host a camel clinic through our vet once a year. It is quite a sight when you look out at 21 camels milling about in one pasture.

I also believe in the power of education and continued learning. I obtained my helicopter type rating last year and someday hope to use that newfound skill to do volunteer search work. I think I got my lifelong learning from my dad. My father always wanted to be a pilot but he pursued a career as an aerospace engineer. As I was moving up through the ranks to be a pilot, I began to take him flying. He was a natural and soon enrolled in ground school. I had the honor of doing all his flight training, including his first solo. That was an incredibly special experience. He got his private pilot certificate and then bought an airplane. He became an accomplished pilot, eventually earning the Airplane Transport Pilot certification, the highest rating a pilot can achieve. I was immensely proud of him, and I treasure the times we shared flying.

People are always remarking that I live an interesting life, and I would agree. However, if I could go back and talk to the young Cheryl Pitzer, I would tell her not to stress out about things that she cannot control and suggest that she have more patience and stop to smell the roses. I would tell my younger self and others just starting out that you really need to be careful about with whom you decide to stir the pot. That person could be your boss someday! Pick your confidants wisely, and be cautious about who you trust. Never let them see you cry — many see tears as a sign of weakness, not as a reaction to frustration. And if you want to be treated as a professional, then act professionally. Most importantly, do not give up. True grit comes from the perseverance to believe in yourself and the sustained fortitude to overcome obstacles.

Every time I go wheels-up and fly off to someplace new and exciting on another of life's great adventures, I remember the simple but perhaps most important Golden Rule and that actions really do speak louder than words.

What details or lessons in this story resonate with me? And why?

How will I apply what I read or learned to my own career or personal life?

" What is success?…To know even one life has breathed easier because you have lived. That is to have succeeded. "
- Ralph Waldo Emerson

Suzanne
Garber

CEO of Gauze
Former Managing Director, Sales
FedEx South America

You've likely heard the phrase, "Lights, camera, action!" My career has mostly focused on the action. In fact, throughout my career, I've had the opportunity to be a global nomad, an entrepreneur, a healthcare advocate, a corporate executive and a filmmaker. That plus a Jesus follower, too.

I owe much of my drive to my parents. They always told me I could do and be anything I wanted. Their confidence in me and their strong advice stuck. In my wallet, I always carry a little card my parents gave me decades ago that reads: "What is success? To laugh often and much; to win the respect of intelligent people and the affection of children; to earn the appreciation of honest critics and endure the betrayal of false friends; to appreciate the beauty; to find the best in others; to leave the world a bit better, whether by a healthy child, a garden patch, or a redeemed social condition; to know even one life has breathed easier because you have lived. This is to have succeeded." Those are the inspiring words of Ralph Waldo Emerson.

My parents modeled my path to success by opening my world to new places, teaching independence and flexibility. My father was an expat, transferred all over the world in his position with General Electric Co. That meant I was exposed to a nomadic lifestyle from an early age. I was reared in Spain, Mexico, Algeria, Egypt, the Dominican Republic and various U.S. states; by the time I was nine years old, I had already filled every page in my first passport.

My own career took a path similar to that of my father when I joined FedEx and was selected to be part of a small group dispatched across the globe. It was a dream come true. Since then, my work has taken me to every continent and over 100 countries. I was afforded many new possibilities, and I proactively sought a different position

True grit surrounds itself with others who have true grit.

— usually of increasing authority — every two to three years at FedEx. That meant moving from Philadelphia to Cincinnati to Washington, D.C., to Miami, to Mexico and then Brazil.

Like many things in life, I learned the most when my path wasn't as smooth, when the unexpected hit. At the age of 33, I was diagnosed with ovarian cancer. Only six weeks married, I was shocked when I heard the news that I had a malignant tumor that needed immediate surgery. I was and continue to be grateful to be married to an amazingly flexible, understanding and supportive husband, Chris, who accompanies and encourages my every move. His grit and tenacity ensured that I received the best care from the best doctors in my city. He tirelessly dogged doctors' offices, demanding faster accessibility so I could receive treatment for the rapidly growing tumor. He spent nights sleeping on the floor in my hospital room to make sure that I got everything I needed. My experience with cancer taught me that everyone needs a champion to navigate life. We cannot do it alone.

Everyone need a champion to navigate life. We cannot do it alone.

But champions don't just live in families. It is important to have champions in our workplaces as well. My champion at FedEx nominated me to interview for an executive level position. I was excited for the opportunity to showcase my skills and talents, but I also knew I did not have as much experience as the other candidates. I did not get that job, but interviewing opened other doors that I had not expected. The interview committee wanted to nurture my career growth and provide an avenue for me to get the experience I would need to advance. They named five locations that needed a director. Only one — Brazil — offered all the experiences I would need to meet future qualifications for advancement. Oh, by the way, a response was needed within 48 hours. Was I interested?

Stepping into something new and risky takes grit, faith and confidence.

Making this decision taught me that stepping into something new and risky takes grit, faith and confidence. Having been to Brazil before, I knew it was a beautiful country but very far away from my family, the company headquarters and my doctors. Would I be forgotten professionally? I didn't speak the language and would not be able to easily communicate with my team. I also worried about my medical care. I would need ongoing support given my history with ovarian cancer. My mind immediately went to the other options, all in either the U.S. or Europe. It was important that I consider my family in this decision-making process as well. Chris and I made a pact that if either of our careers got in the way of our marriage, our marriage would win. Nothing is more important than our relationship. I wondered if Chris would want to move again? This would be the fifth move in our sixth year of marriage. I was aware that half of all expatriate assignments fail due to family reasons. When I approached him with the choices I had been presented, he told me he would fast and pray to make the right decision for us as a family. Within 48 hours, we made the decision for Brazil, and moving there continues to be one of the best decisions of our lives. Why? Mostly because of all the growth I experienced personally and professionally.

The language barrier was my first challenge. I hired a private tutor to coach me 12 hours a week until I could speak reliably with employees and clients, and I asked that the team talk to me only in Portuguese. By month four, I gave my first full meeting in Portuguese — with a few glitches and guffaws, much to the glee of the local team. As for the next challenge of thinking I'd be forgotten professionally, I was able to work on projects I never would have had the opportunity to experience had I stayed in the U.S. or gone to a developed region like Europe. We opened new markets in Colombia and Ecuador, started new flight routes in Uruguay and Argentina and began negotiations for the acquisition of a premier Brazilian domestic delivery provider. Along the way, my team and I racked up multiple awards, including several trips to the coveted President's Club, an elite designation earned by less than five percent of the FedEx sales population.

Chris and I got plugged into the community, feeding the homeless every Friday night along with a caravan of other FedEx colleagues. Chris, who had been the U.S. Army Corps Wrestling Champion in the 1990s, was asked to join the coveted Alliance Jiu Jitsu Team headed by Brazilian Jiu Jitsu World Champion Fabio Gurgel. Chris went on to win the Brazilian national championship for his age and belt class just a year later. And, from a health perspective, the quality of care I received in Brazil was outstanding. What I thought would be challenges to my marriage, my health and my career actually benefited all three. The experience of living and working in Brazil was a springboard for my career and strengthened relationships in ways I could never have dreamed.

Fast forward a few years and another pivotal event in my life occurred while traveling in the Middle East. I couldn't catch my breath, and I wasn't sure if I was having a heart attack or a panic attack. Either way, I knew I did not want to get sick there. I did not speak the language where I was, and I had reasons to doubt the quality of healthcare I might receive. I returned to the U.S., assuming I would be in much better hands, but then I was misdiagnosed multiple times. As it turned out, I was born with a rare, congenital heart defect that required open heart surgery to save my life. Having never known about this defect meant I had been misdiagnosed since birth.

While recovering in the hospital from my major surgery, Chris and I researched and strategized a business plan to help people who get sick outside their home countries. We learned that out of 1.4 billion international travelers, between 10-40 percent become ill while abroad. That is nearly half a billion people! I know that scenario well. You see, I've not only been sick in the Middle East and had oncology treatments in Brazil, but I had an appendectomy in Spain, bronchitis in Greece, malaria in Mexico and seen orthopedists in Singapore. I've probably been sick in more countries than most people have ever visited for fun.

Out of the painful nights in the hospital, we created our company, Gauze, now the world's leading database of hospitals outside the United States. Through a mobile app, Gauze informs and connects people with appropriate health care facilities for when they get sick outside their home countries. Chris and I also wrote a pilot script for a film that would educate others on the realities, rewards and risks of international healthcare. Within six months of leaving the hospital, I left my corporate job. I directed and produced "GAUZE: Unraveling Global Healthcare," an award-winning PBS documentary that highlights my journey to 24 countries, 174 hospitals and interviews with 65 international healthcare experts, medical journal editors and hospital CEOs. The entire filming process took three years and was something I would have never thought I would do.

True Grit surrounds itself with others who have true grit.

Today my mission and learning continue to grow. I want to change the landscape of the health care system in the U.S. To do that properly, I am currently pursuing a Doctor of Science in Health Care Leadership at the top-ranked University of Alabama at Birmingham where I am working on several papers in health policy and marketing with a particular focus on health care transparency and accessibility. I am going to combine my knowledge of international health care systems with my experience with efficient delivery systems courtesy of FedEx, toward increasing price transparency, reducing medical bankruptcies and improving overall access to care for all Americans. The colleagues in my cohort — several U.S.-based hospital CEOs, pharmaceutical executives and esteemed clinical providers — are among the most courageous, generous and grittiest people I know. They regularly risk their lives to save others. I am grateful and humbled to be among them, for true grit surrounds itself with others who have true grit.

True Grit opts for kindness and humility, even when you don't feel like it.

Through all of life's turns, I have taken the power of grit and perseverance to achieve my personal and career goals. But I have also learned a lot about engaging with people. Throughout my professional travels and experiences, particularly those in Latin America, I learned just how impactful respect and kindness can be. While some may decry my actions as not sticking up for myself or giving in to perceived discrimination, I found it best to observe first before trying to change deep-seated cultural norms. Having male 'stand ins' during customer meetings meant humbling myself, assimilating into the culture and ultimately, earning both the business and respect of prospective and current clients. Such an attitude almost always caught clients and employees alike off guard. It also quickly diffused tense situations. True grit opts for kindness and humility, even when you don't feel like it. And just as I learned early in my career, life shouldn't be done alone. People, champions, mentors, family and friends impact our lives. The nomadic life broadens paradigms but moving around meant I rarely developed deep roots in a geographic area. Thus, I learned the value of maintaining friendships in each place I lived. This required using technology to stay in touch with each of those friends around the world was and is important to me and was reflected by the many cards that lined my hospital room during my bout with cancer.

My advice to women regardless of age or career is to take risks, step outside your comfort zones and believe beyond the limits of what you can see now.

Every opportunity afforded to me enriches my life — especially the ones that are not the most obviously attractive. Too often, we stay in our comfortable lane, avoiding risk. My advice to women regardless of age or career is to take risks, step outside your comfort zones and believe beyond the limits of what you can see now. Doing things you may not want to do is uncomfortable, even painful. Yet, like a rubber band, life is most impactful when it's stretched.

What details or lessons in this story resonate with me? And why?

How will I apply what I read or learned to my own career or personal life?

> *" If you're always trying to be normal, you will never know how amazing you can be. "*
> *- Maya Angelou*

Ramona

Hood

CEO
FedEx Custom Critical

My childhood included many challenges, but it was rich in love and support. When I came into the world, it was a time of joy for my family but also a painful reminder of tragedy. My father, Raymond Kidd, had drowned the previous August. I was blessed with my name to remind my grandparents of their child — the youngest of four — who did not live to see me born.

My goals from as far back as I can remember were driven by resilience and ambition to honor the dad I never knew. I was always encouraged to dream big — my mother frequently reminding me to, "Reach for the moon and land on the stars." My dreams were big, but they were not specific. I wanted to be "successful" but wasn't sure what success looked like.

When I joined Roberts Express, which later became FedEx Custom Critical, I was a 19-year-old single mother looking for a position with regular hours and a steady paycheck. I didn't know then that this entry-level receptionist job would be the foundation of a rewarding career and lead to a historic milestone for our company.

For over two decades, I intentionally grew and gained experience within the company from safety to sales, marketing, operations and logistics. I wanted to learn and make sure I had well-rounded experience to fully understand various positions that make up what we do as a corporation. Those experiences taught me that it was important to stretch myself and get comfortable with the uncomfortable. I took on tasks and responsibilities that were outside my comfort zone and even a little intimidating. But entering each new area allowed me to add value with my own unique perspective and gain learning to be a more valuable employee.

True Grit is a way of being. It is someone who is courageous in their actions and thoughts. It is someone who takes risks and falls forward with failures.

This year, when I accepted my current role as president and CEO of FedEx Custom Critical, I called my daughters, Mariah and Kayla, to share the news: their mom was the first African American female CEO at FedEx. I will never forget Mariah's response: "Does that mean you just made history?" The feelings I had at that moment are indescribable. Reflecting now, I see several factors that fueled my success.

A strong leader is frequently challenged with the priorities of both professional and personal lives. When one gets out of sync, it affects everything. As a single mother and an executive, I weigh professional and personal decisions thoroughly to understand the impact and trade-off for not just me, but for my daughters as well.

> **Taking a moment to savor a success is worthwhile but knowing where we can improve helps us get stronger and keep moving.**

Another important truth I embrace and share often with Mariah and Kayla is one of humble assurance — the balance of sharing doubts and vulnerabilities just as willingly as we tout our successes. We are all human, so leveraging our strengths along with acknowledging opportunities and weaknesses is critical to growth. Taking a moment to savor a success is worthwhile, but knowing where we can improve helps us get stronger and keep moving.

I also believe in mentorship. Though my mother was my first mentor, I credit my early career launch to a group of friends and mentors who became my own personal board of directors. They took the time and interest to see my potential when I didn't have the experience to see it myself. They also challenged me to think about possibilities with confidence, to not sell myself short. My mentors encouraged me to never stop learning and be prepared for opportunities when they come along. It was not easy, but I earned a business management degree from Walsh University and then an Executive MBA from Case Western Reserve University while working full-time and raising two daughters. Virginia Addicott was a mentor, boss, leader and a sponsor. She was the first professional person who asked me what my career goals were. "Being successful" was not an acceptable answer for Virginia! Kevin McClellan was also an advocate. He inspired me to think long term and taught me the value of listening and advising honestly. Both Virginia and Kevin believed in my potential and encouraged me to think strategically and outside the box.

Most importantly, I learned from mentors that helping people be their best selves and investing in others is a lifelong gift. Whether a fellow employee, customer or a friend just starting on their career path, we each have the power to make a difference. I am now a mentor myself because I want to make an impact. That's why I am especially proud to be a part of the FedEx Women in Leadership program that exposes women to other leaders and new ideas and offers encouragement to set and reach goals.

I am also an advocate for education and learning and support many learning programs at the local and national levels. Investing in lifelong learning is like sowing seeds. It is so rewarding to watch children grow and flourish. I am a member of a local board in Ohio whose goal is to improve literacy among African American children, from cradle to career. I support programs that restore reading centers to help children have access to books and tutoring so they can become better and more enthusiastic readers. Two more of my favorite programs are the United Way, which helps so many across a broad array of needs, and the Dolly Parton Foundation, which encourages literacy by providing books to children across America.

The truth is, I haven't stopped learning. Someone once described me as a sponge, and I take that as a compliment. Learning is one reason I love to travel. My daughters often travel with me. On one journey before a business trip, we enjoyed a memorable adventure in Paris and Rome. And when I continued my business trip, Mariah and Kayla flew home solo. Yes, mom worried, but all went smoothly. We created great family memories and experienced other countries and cultures, but my girls also gained a new confidence in being able to do something they had never done before.

Learning is a part of daily life at FedEx Custom Critical, which specializes in time sensitive surface-expedite freight delivery shipments. We also serve as an intermediary, arranging shipments of freight for customers with a wide variety of transportation needs. My team never has a dull day. We have transported ancient artifacts, delivered concert equipment for world-renowned rock bands and carried sports equipment for the Super Bowl and national basketball championships. We even helped deliver holiday gifts to "The Oprah Winfrey Show" for its "Oprah's Favorite Things" segment, and we made sure actress Hilary Swank received her organic wedding cake from Mexico on time.

Other things we do may not be front line news or glamorous but are everything to those who need them. For example, one of the company's biggest opportunities for growth is in servicing the health care industry. Consider medical devices or pharmaceuticals for instance: the customer and the recipient need to know that the package stays at the necessary temperature through the entire delivery journey. Lives depend on us doing it right.

Over the past 28 years, that undefined dream of success I had as a child has evolved. I now define success as being able to have a positive effect on other people, helping them to grow and reach their full potential. I challenge every leader at FedEx to look beyond yourself to find fulfillment that comes from helping others succeed. Like Maya Angelou, I know that mentoring to "amazing" is an investment worth making.

What details or lessons in this story resonate with me? And why?

How will I apply what I read or learned to my own career or personal life?

" Live as if you were to die tomorrow. Learn as if you were to live forever. "
- Mahatma Gandhi

Jill

Brannon

Executive Vice President,
Chief Sales Officer
FedEx Corporation

When I was a child, I had some lofty goals. I wanted to be adventurous and travel the world. I wanted to remain true to myself, do what is right and learn something new every day along the way. So far, I have been fortunate in life to have experienced so many of my childhood dreams. From these basic beginnings, I set forward on a path to find a global company with opportunities to grow and discover and one where I could excel.

That might sound like a tall order for a girl born to a family of mostly farmers and millworkers in North Carolina. But, I know some of those lofty goals came from my dad who encouraged my siblings and me to think for ourselves and dream big. With his military background, a proud Korean War veteran, my father believed in us and knew that we could achieve practically anything to which we set our minds. He and my mom were our first mentors, and the lessons they taught are still with me.

I admit I am a "daddy's girl." We have a unique bond, and he was the first person that challenged me to think critically — to sell an idea or defend a point. He loved teaching us how to debate. He took one side of the argument and then required us to research the other position and prove our cases. Those fun debates around the family table taught us so much about preparing before making a decision. We learned about organization and negotiation and how to present an argument with confidence. Most importantly, we learned to recognize that there is always more than one position or opinion that should be considered with any issue. That lesson taught me to be open to inclusive views to achieve the best outcomes.

My mother was a stickler for making time for family — especially sitting down at the table together for dinners. We talked about our day, our interests

True grit: being true to who you are with sheer determination, tenacity and positivity regardless of the tough things that might happen along the way.

and what was going on in our lives. That time made each of us feel important and assured us that our parents cared about what we were involved in. I remember laughter around that table as well. We had fun as a family and often used humor. Mark Twain so aptly said, "Humor is the great thing, the saving thing. The minute it crops up, all our irritations and resentments slip away and a sunny spirit takes their place."

I was the first in our family to go to college. Thanks to scholarships, I graduated from Lenoir-Rhyne University in Hickory, N.C., with degrees in International Business and French. That is where my dream of global travel first became a reality. Taking advantage of the school's study-abroad programs, I had the opportunity to visit other countries, learn about other cultures and broaden my perspective. Those experiences inspired me to dream even bigger.

My first job at FedEx was in operations, working on the dock in the hub from 5 p.m. to 5 a.m., seven days on, seven days off. The schedule and work were not easy, but it was one of the best ways to start at the company because I was able to learn and appreciate the core of our business and the magic that happens each night in our hubs, terminals and stations. After three years in operations in two states, my manager suggested a change that aligned with my strengths and career goals. He recognized my passion and love for a challenge and suggested that I move into a sales role. I am confident the experiences I had competing to win debates with my dad helped me prepare for it in so many ways. I guess you could say I "grew up" at FedEx with colleagues and mentors. I earned a hands-on professional education that took me to many geographies and led to personal moves, learning new insights along the way. Now three decades into my career at FedEx, I am honored to lead an organization of more than 15,000 team members worldwide.

When I am asked about how to succeed in business, particularly as a woman, I never have a single answer. Some luck and timing may be part of the equation, but the core of achieving dreams is about being focused, passionate, authentic, adaptable and working hard. A leader at any level always has a clear vision, surrounds themselves with the best possible team, delivers results and celebrates success. A true leader is confident enough to take risks and embraces people by building individuals and teams. And a leader possesses true grit: being true to who you are with sheer determination, tenacity and positivity regardless of the tough things that might happen along the way.

Often when we lose sight of our destination, we need to simplify complicated problems and tasks, more effectively assess and analyze them and then better address them. My son, Jake, had a couple of favorite stories as a child, and I often adapt their messages for various audiences when I speak. Simple visuals and stories resonate with all ages and help us remember important principles. One of Jake's favorites tells about a humpback whale, Humphrey, who lost his way on the annual migration from Alaska to Mexico and became stranded in San Francisco Bay. The big animal — 45 feet long and weighing 41 tons — apparently became confused by all the noise and activity in the area and lost the way to his destination. He was in real danger of dying, trapped in the rivers and estuaries around the bay for 16 days. Rescuers were finally able to lure Humphrey back out to sea by playing the recorded sounds of humpbacks feeding and frolicking. The audio, played at high levels, covered all the other noise and distractions that had kept Humphrey from finding his true course. Of course, the lesson is to focus on things that are most important — the signals above the noise. Let go or deprioritize the distractions that come up every day. Keep your eye on the goal, and stay tuned to the signal above the noise. It may even be life-saving.

I also recommend being intentional with time — owning your calendar and how you spend your day. If we're not intentional about allocating time, it will be allocated for us and leave little room for the highest priorities like family, or even quiet time to think and recharge to be your best self. A typical day for me includes an early morning run outdoors to keep healthy and fit; meditating and being grateful; and blocking time to simply think, clear my head, plan, prioritize and organize. My faith is very important to me and has helped me to stay centered. I run with no music. It's just me and nature. It provides a time to step away from the "noise" of the world and focus on the important things — the signals above the noise.

> **Taking the time to let people know that they are important and that you are truly paying attention is critical to communication and connecting.**

Another simple concept that I learned as a child and still practice today is the power of please and thank you. Taking the time to let people know that they are important and that you are truly paying attention is critical to communication and connecting. That is one reason I always strive to be an active listener. It's amazing what you can learn from others when you take time to really listen. I enjoy mentoring, and during these sessions, it's so important to practice active listening and ask effective questions — yes, a sales skill too. I am curious about human nature and try to understand what really motivates a mentee — what is their passion? Once we identify what truly brings the mentee joy, it makes it easier to apply the person's talents and skills toward these driving forces behind success and happiness. One of my true delights is seeing those I have helped along the way get promoted and celebrate their accomplishments.

As a female executive, the road has not always been easy. I have experienced some trade-offs but learned to develop creative ways to balance home and work and stay connected to my family. I have a wonderful spouse, Bill, and son who have supported me in so many ways. I was older than many women at the time I had my son. It was natural that I felt guilty having to travel so much when Jake was young. When he was three, I accepted my first international position with the company. By the time he was six, I was traveling extensively, often gone weeks out of the month. Of course, in the spirit of owning my calendar, I did my best to ensure I was with family for those moments that matter. But, when I was traveling, we learned to make the most of it and recognized that the quality of time we spent together was the important thing. We used Skype so we could see each other from hotel rooms all over the world. I would tell Jake where I was, and he would locate the city on a globe. I made it a point to bring back artwork from places I visited, and he always looked forward to learning more about the artist, the country and the culture from which it came. I would buy toys or souvenir items I thought he would like so he could collect them. That allowed him to feel like he was a part of my journeys, too.

When Jake got older, we began to travel as a family. I wanted Jake to experience new cultures, people and traditions firsthand. Before he finished high school, my son had been to each of the continents except Antarctica. We even learned to speak a bit of the different languages of the places we visited. I might not have been able to be there for some of his special moments, but I was able to expose him to a whole new perspective and broaden his experiences at an early age. And what memories we have created together as a family! We thoroughly enjoyed living in Amsterdam for a while and learned to know and love the city. We have experienced the wonderful food of Italy, the art and culture of France, the stunning scenery of Australia, a night safari in the Dubai desert and a dance around bonfires to the beat of drums with locals in Africa. We have enjoyed memorable and spiritual experiences in Japan, China, Iceland, Egypt, the Galapagos Islands — each of which gave me a new awakening and a strong sense of inner peace.

"Harold and the Purple Crayon" is another of Jake's favorite childhood stories. In this inspiring book, a young boy goes for a nighttime walk, carrying a purple crayon. He uses the crayon to draw his own magical, fanciful world, a landscape of wonder and excitement. If he wanted an adventure populated by dragons, all he had to do was use the purple crayon to draw some, but he could always return safely to his bed after the quest was complete. This wonderful children's story shows how we can use creativity to relate to others and create our own paths. Of course, purple is very relatable to all of us at FedEx, symbolizing how we work together as a team and with purple passion.

Today, I urge all women to take out that purple crayon and live your dreams with passion, humor, authenticity, creativity, a learning mindset, determination and grit. Looking back to the lofty dreams of my childhood, I can say with confidence that I have achieved what I set out to do as a little girl, and more. I am living my dream every day and look forward to my next adventures.

What details or lessons in this story resonate with me? And why?

How will I apply what I read or learned to my own career or personal life?

Peggy
Carrera

Managing Director,
Transportation
FedEx Ground

True grit is strength, courage and resolve.

> *" To whom much is given, much will be required. "*
> *- Luke 12:48*

To me, true grit is strength, courage, and resolve. Do I have true grit? Absolutely! I am presented with challenges every day that require me to demonstrate that fact. Leading through any crisis, minor or major, makes me stronger and more tenacious.

The truth is, I had the opportunity very early in my life to develop inner strength and resolve. My parents migrated from Colombia, South America, to the U.S. after they were married. Not long after, they separated. Mom and I moved back to Colombia where I spent most of my childhood growing up on an island.

It was a good life where we were devoted to the church, family and community. I spent a lot of my childhood with my grandparents. Though we were not wealthy, I never lacked for anything. That was because my mom worked hard to provide for me as well as for her parents and siblings.

Then something happened at an early age that required me to call upon that supply of true grit. When I was seven years old, I was seriously injured in a motorcycle accident while riding with my dad. I remember very little from the accident and woke up in a hospital shocked to see the obvious scars on my face. I was in the hospital for a long time and when I was finally released, I did not want to return to school. In fact, I did not want to see anyone or have anyone see me. As I feared, when I did go back to school, some of my classmates laughed and called me "scarface." Surprisingly, it was mostly the girls who were so cruel. The boys were very protective. One way I overcame the bullying was to focus on my studies. I excelled in school. Many years later, I decided to take motorcycle-riding lessons to help overcome the fear caused by the accident. It was especially difficult since I had never driven a big bike like that myself. But I did it, and facing that challenge is an accomplishment of which I am very proud.

While growing up in Colombia I also became aware of the true need that exists in our world. I saw children who lacked even basics. I knew then that I would do everything I could to help and protect these children. "Annie" was one of my favorite shows as a child, so my dream was to build an orphanage. Today, I proudly support charities devoted to needy children and I personally sponsor children back in Colombia to help them get through school and college. I do not share this to seek praise or recognition — I share because I want a better life for children and their families and hope my dream will inspire others to see their own blessings and want to help others as well.

After graduating high school, my parents reunited and we moved back to the U.S. The transition was an experience in and of itself. I remembered little of my earlier childhood here and, of course, I missed my family and friends back in Colombia. I was not sure where I wanted to go to college and was undecided about my career path. I considered law and other choices, but graduated with a degree in industrial engineering. I have never regretted that choice.

Early on in my career, I gained a lot of experience in a start-up company. It taught me about business, leadership and the unique issues that stem from rapid growth. I also had the opportunity to travel throughout the U.S. which reinforced the importance of aligning values and goals across all aspects of a business. I have been at FedEx for over 20 years and am now managing director of Transportation. It's been an amazing ride in various leadership roles, ranging from engineering to operations management.

Be intentional about personal and professional learning.

One of the most powerful lessons I have learned throughout my career is the importance of being intentional about personal and professional learning. In each professional role I have held, I sought out growth opportunities — willingly transforming myself every step of the way. The FedEx Global Leadership Corps (GLC) program is one example. I was honored to be a part of GLC — an immersive leadership development experience. The program sends FedEx team members to emerging countries to work with government, nonprofit groups or private organizations on critical local projects. My group was deployed to Sofia, Bulgaria. I knew very little about Bulgaria at the time. I like to think of myself as a global citizen, but Bulgaria was not on my radar. I doubt I could have even found it on a world map. Our client was Human in the Loop (HiTL), which is a social enterprise that trains and employs refugees to deliver services to the artificial intelligence and machine learning industry. The refugees are primarily from Syria, Iraq and Afghanistan. The founder is a young woman from Bulgaria who is not a refugee nor is she related to one. She is driven by a passion for human rights. At such a young age, she is more of an inspiration than she realizes.

This experience allowed me to recognize the significance of human connection. HiTL is an amazing organization with a group of phenomenal individuals who, because of war, had to flee their homes. They are in unfamiliar places with different languages and religions. Sadly, they often face unfounded discrimination by those who don't understand or want them in their country. Through HiTL, these individuals found someone in Bulgaria who believes in them. In return, there is strength, connection and loyalty. Once you get to know diverse groups of people in a meaningful way, you realize that we all have a unifying human connection.

On the last day of the program, we had the chance to present our deliverables and recommendation as a GLC cohort. The common theme was efficiency and Quality Driven Management — a way of life at FedEx. At the ceremony, an alumnus from the Junior Achievement team — who is from Bulgaria — shared that he had the opportunity to visit the U.S. where he attended a conference sponsored by FedEx. He reported that Fred Smith had given a speech at the event. He told the group of Junior Achievers that you may forget what you learn at your job, but the relationships you build along the way will remain. That statement resonated with the young man and still does with me. The relationships I built in Bulgaria are some of the most meaningful in my career.

Visiting a new country also teaches the value of being open to new perspectives and not remaining within the limits of our own lives or situations. While visiting Bulgaria, I immersed myself in the culture, thirsty to drink in as much as I could. When I first arrived in Sofia, all I saw was gray buildings, graffiti and a depressed country, remnants of what I perceived to be the Communist influence. When I left, I did not see one gray building and the graffiti had turned into works of art. The trees were green, the sun was bright and the birds were all happily chirping. Reflecting, and looking beyond the surface, I realized that Bulgaria is actually a very happy country, now proudly beyond a history of oppression, struggle and war.

Be willing to evolve and look for new perspectives.

I vowed to learn at least 30 new words during my month in Bulgaria, one new word a day. At the emigration counter, I could not wait to show off my newly learned Bulgarian words. The officer was so impressed that he started a conversation. I laughed and stopped him, reminding him I only knew 30 words, a word for every day I had been in his beautiful country. That impressed him even more. He told me, "There are people who are here for 20 years and don't even know one word!" My learning from GLC has stayed with me throughout my career. Being willing to evolve and look for new perspectives is something I try to teach others, especially as it relates to overcoming gender challenges. I recall when I first became a senior manager in New York, I was the only female manager in my peer group of 19 senior managers. So, I started a women's leadership forum to explore why more women were not stepping forward to seek management roles. The overwhelming response — no one had ever asked them. No one had tapped them on the shoulder and invited them to go after an open management position. Amazingly, that is still, in my view, the main reason women are hesitant to compete. I made it my mission to mentor and sponsor women for leadership roles and help them move past real or perceived notions that they cannot advance. I helped them see that taking the initiative to grow with confidence makes a difference. I taught them that many barriers can be removed by simply changing the way we communicate or by tailoring the message to the people who need to hear it. When I left New York, the number of women holding management roles had tripled.

I am encouraged to see barriers to gender equality being removed every day. I was thrilled recently when the U.S. President held a special event at the White House to honor the transportation industry. The driver who took one of our trucks to the ceremony was a female. I cannot describe the pride of not only seeing one of our FedEx vehicles on the front lawn of the White House, but also having a woman recognized in a job once totally dominated by men.

> **We grow by being an advocate. We help ourselves when we help people. We transform while we are encouraging others to transform.**

Everything — in business and in life — is about leadership. We grow by being an advocate. We help ourselves when we help people. We transform while we are encouraging others to transform. We grow when we influence and empower other people to do what they need to do to excel. As females, we must speak up and let our light shine. Earlier in my career, I learned that being curious and asking questions gets the best results. I attended many meetings with senior officers and made sure I left with the answers: What are we really hoping to get out of these meetings? What do the numbers and lists mean? Are they actionable or relevant? Just by asking these types of questions, we began to get stronger and more efficient outcomes from the meetings. At the same time, those senior officers began to take notice of the girl with the accent with all the questions. And that bold curiosity led to more leadership opportunities for me.

As I reflect on what success looks like, I never think of my achievements as my own. It is always a team effort, at work or at home. My success is measured by the success of my team. It is in the healthy balance that we are at our best.

Early in my professional life, my career and advancement were the drivers in my life. I have learned as I mature to create space for both work and family. My family at home may get tired of me always talking about Quality Driven Management and attempting to apply the principles at home. But I remind them, it works at FedEx and it works in every other aspect of our lives, too. It's simple: view failures as opportunities and find the root cause of a problem. Once you know the real problem, find a solution.

My family has always been supportive, and my daughter does a wonderful job of keeping both of her parents grounded. Isabella is 12 now. She loves to cook and to dance. She even makes me get up and dance, too, but I mostly just make a fool of myself. She also enjoys travel and is a great travel partner for me. She is so very curious and wants to learn about everything she sees. That is sometimes a challenge for me because I admit I do not know all the answers to her questions. Isabella spends summers in Colombia and thrives on experiencing different cultures.

When I was pregnant with Isabella, I was determined to raise a child who would leave the world a better place. To be more than she thought she could be. I would make certain my baby would never have what I call an "impoverished mind," resulting from low expectations and the belief that difficult things are not possible. Instead, I teach Isabella to be willing to compete, to have a tenacity and grit in all things she does.

So, what advice would I give a young woman who aspires for success in business? Be curious, always look for growth both personally and professionally. Let your light shine with confidence and humility. Look for the need in the world and try to make an impact. And most importantly, be yourself. Don't try to be someone you are not. But to do that, you must first discover who you are — not what family, friends, colleagues or bosses think or expect. You must be aware of your strengths and dreams and embrace what you want for yourself, what you hope to offer others and to your company.

Be the person you want others to know you to be.

What details or lessons in this story resonate with me? And why?

How will I apply what I read or learned to my own career or personal life?

Jane

Amaba

Vice President, Finance
FedEx Services

True grit is the perseverance to never give up despite the obstacles in your path.

" Courage doesn't always roar. Sometimes courage is the quiet voice at the end of the day saying, 'I will try again tomorrow.' "
- Mary Anne Radmacher

I spent many hours thinking about my story and what moment or experience to share that would be the perfect example of "true grit." The more I reflected, I realized that for me, grit is not about one moment. It's about an accumulation of challenges, opportunities, priorities and people all woven together to make me the person I am today. Now, just like family stories that are passed down to younger generations, I hope that my story will teach and inspire other women to dig deep and find the grit and path that uniquely defines them.

I grew up an only child in a rural manufacturing town in Virginia. My dad was a factory worker, and we lived near my grandparents' farm. Because my parents grew up during the Depression, I was taught to be frugal. I learned that since we never know what tomorrow will bring, we should be prepared by saving. Counting pennies in my childhood was a prelude to my career in financial planning.

When I was born, my mother quit her job in a doctor's office, and my dad began working double shifts so she could stay home. Every summer when the factory closed for two weeks, we spent that time at my grandparents' farm. A farmer's day starts early and ends late. Summer on the farm included baling hay, chopping and stacking firewood for winter and building fences. It was hot, sweaty and dusty, and the barn smelled like cows. While I would have preferred to be sitting on a blanket in the shade reading a Nancy Drew book, there was always work to be done. Those days on the farm taught me the importance of a strong work ethic and showed me that work never ends, so it is best to choose a career you enjoy.

Once when I was eight, my dad told me he needed help to move a table upstairs from our basement. I took about two steps and put down my end complaining, "This is heavy!" My dad responded,

"Of course it is, that's why I need help. Now pick it up, and let's move." His just do it attitude to muscle through tough times was the way that I learned to approach life.

My mother went back to work when I was 10, which meant I needed to be independent and self-reliant as a latchkey kid. Watching my mom gave me an appreciation for what it takes to balance work and home. Even after a full day of work, she had family dinner on the table every night at exactly 6 p.m. She was a great role model, demonstrating incredible organization and time management.

Before I entered high school, the zoning for our school districts changed. My new classmates were from an affluent area. They were children of doctors, engineers, and business owners. All of them aspired to go to college. I had been one of the top students in my rural school, but now there was a higher bar for achievement. The new competition was a driver to push myself. I decided even if I was not necessarily the smartest in my class, I could work the hardest and still be successful. Dedication in high school led to being class president, cheerleading captain, graduating seventh in my class and early acceptance at Virginia Tech. I am grateful for my high school friends who challenged me to work harder and be better.

After graduating from college, I took a consulting job in Washington, D.C., and began working toward an MBA at night. The schedule and commute were brutal, so I made a decision — one very unpopular with my parents — to leave my job and study full-time. I then began school at the University of Georgia — a place where I knew no one. Shortly before graduation, during the interview process with FedEx, I learned about an amazing benefit of working for the company — jumpseating. I could fly anywhere in the world for free! I set a goal to visit all 50 states. I have now accomplished that — twice!

On my very first day at FedEx, I met a coworker on a temporary assignment. After a few months, he changed industries and moved out of state. Two years later, I married him. By marrying Ben, I became not only a wife but a step-mother, bringing joy as well as an abundance of patience and grit. Since I loved my job, I made a case for a remote position. I became the first telecommuter in my division and made sure my experience paved the way for others seeking the same opportunity.

For almost two years, I drove five hours each way, one week a month, to stay connected at the office. The rest of the month, I worked from home supporting international projects, which meant taking global conference calls around the clock. Ben took a new role that allowed geographic flexibility, and I assumed we would move back to Memphis. Then, a management job posted in Miami, and my options suddenly expanded. When I learned that the Miami position already had a strong candidate, I decided not to even try. The next week, I mentioned the job and my decision to a colleague, and he strongly urged me to apply. I did, and I got the job. Several valuable lessons here: be confident in your abilities; don't give up on an opportunity so easily; and never underestimate the value of a supportive and encouraging network of friends.

We loved living in Miami — a city of unique culture and diversity. Everything was falling into place including excitement about expanding our family. What was anticipated to be one of the most joyful days of my life sadly turned out to be one of the worst. Expecting to hear "It's a boy!" or "It's a girl!" during an 18-week ultrasound, I was devastated to learn that due to a total loss of amniotic fluid, there would be no happy bundle of joy arriving five months later. Losing our little girl resulted in sadness I have never known. I had not shared the news of my first pregnancy with coworkers, so I returned to work and fell back into my normal routine. Somehow, I summoned the grit to move forward.

The road to motherhood was not an easy one. Each subsequent pregnancy ended earlier than the last. After many losses but unyielding perseverance, I was finally pregnant — with twin boys!

When my twins were five weeks old, my boss shared that a director position was open and encouraged me to apply. The timing was not ideal, but thankfully, the boys allowed me to get enough sleep the night before my interview, and I got the job. Another lesson: don't wait for perfect timing. There is no such thing.

I knew there would be challenges in taking on a big job with two infants. Integrating a career and family is never easy, especially with a husband that travels extensively for work. But not only did I have an amazing team at work, I was also fortunate to find a wonderful nanny to care for my boys. I never once worried about their safety and happiness, so I was able to focus and thrive in my new position. I always stress the importance of knowing when you need help and having the confidence to ask for it with those that I mentor. A strong and robust support network with multiple levels of contingencies is an important factor for success — and sanity.

My grandmother Gertrude had a framed quote hanging above the sink in her farmhouse: "God grant me the serenity to accept the things I cannot change, the courage to change the things I can, and the wisdom to know the difference." As a working mom I had to learn to focus on the things I could control and not waste time worrying about things I couldn't. That leads to difficult choices sometimes, such as balancing my work schedule with the kids' school events. I was not able to attend everything, so I focused on events where my kids were uniquely recognized.

After six years as a director, I was encouraged to compete for a vice president position. I interviewed as the only outsider and only woman. Statistically, I had a low shot at getting the position, but I did, and we relocated to Memphis. Only weeks after moving, my six-year-old son mentioned that he hated physical education class, which seemed a strange comment for an active boy. He told us that he was the slowest runner in the class, and it hurt when he sat cross-legged and he had trouble getting to his feet. We took him to an expert rheumatologist where he was diagnosed with juvenile dermatomyositis (JM), a rare disease with no known cure. My life suddenly turned upside-down. I had to balance the challenges of a new city and job without the support network that I had in Miami, while learning about a rare disease. As a twin, my son had the opportunity to participate in a special study to learn more about the genetics of JM. We spent several days at the National Institutes of Health in Maryland for assessments and tests. One night as we returned to the Children's Inn, a facility that provided free lodging to patients and their families, dinner was served by volunteers from a large company. I have never been so grateful and humbled as I stood in line that night, exhausted, scared, uncertain of the future, but welcomed by a group of compassionate volunteers.

As the recipient of that generosity when we needed it the most, I appreciate the value of the FedEx Family House, which provides shelter and meals to families with children receiving treatment at LeBonheur Children's Hospital. Our family is a faithful supporter of this house, as we remember what it was like to be on the other side of that food line. Two years of treatment led to JM remission, and our son returned to being an active boy.

Months later another heartbreak. I remember running out of a meeting when I got the phone call that there had been an accident. As a mother, nothing takes more grit than telling your bleeding, bruised, and swollen-faced child, "It's going to be okay," even when you are not sure. The ride to the hospital felt like forever, and the X-rays and diagnosis for reconstructive surgery made for a very long night. While I can talk about grit, I now know that my son has it. He is strong beyond his years, and I am proud to be his mother.

Once the challenges of my son's illness and accident were behind us, we faced another medical surprise, with my husband, Ben. I am blessed to have married an amazing and strong man; he is my soul mate. He is truly larger than life, seemingly invincible. That is why it was such a shock when we learned that he had a major heart issue that would require immediate open-heart surgery to replace a valve. The defect could have killed him in weeks if not repaired. He spent nine days in the ICU. There were times we were not sure he was going to make it, yet, he made a full recovery. The titanium plate in his chest and zipper scar on his chest are visible reminders of what true grit means.

As famously quoted in the movie "Forrest Gump," "Life is like a box of chocolates. You never know what you are going to get." This was never more true than the phone call I received from the dermatologist's office after an initial visit and cautionary biopsy. "You have melanoma," my doctor said. It was business planning season in the finance department, and I did not have time for cancer, but 23 stitches later I became a survivor.

Don't look at challenges as barriers; see them as problems to be solved.

I don't look at challenges as barriers; I see them as problems to be solved. To me, true grit is the perseverance to never give up despite the obstacles in your path. I have a high bar for what difficult looks like, as I have had many role models to learn from, who all persevered in the midst of challenge.

My father worked at a factory job for more than 35 years but never took a sick day, or even an aspirin. At 85, he cut wood outside in freezing temperatures because he enjoyed it. I was sure he would live to be 100, but then came an unexpected diagnosis. A few months later, I held his hand as he took his last breath and died of pancreatic cancer, known to be one of the most excruciatingly painful cancers. He never once complained or asked for pain medicine. He had true grit.

My grandmother Thelma grew up on a farm. One of nine children, she was the cook and caretaker for the family. Before she passed away — at age 98 — she got down on her hands and knees and showed me what it takes to get the kitchen floor really clean.

My great-grandmother gave birth to 15 children, buried six as children, then watched three sons leave to fight in wars to protect our country. She lost her eyesight from an illness but left a legacy of a strong family bond.

My grandfather, her oldest, was still working when he passed away at 91.

My in-laws were immigrants that came to the U.S. to build a better life. But it wasn't easy. While her military husband was deployed overseas, my mother-in-law had to work multiple jobs while raising four children.

My father, several uncles, and many cousins served our country in various branches of the military. When I hear their stories of danger, bravery, honor and near-death, I am grateful that they chose grit.

All of these strong women and men in my life have experienced significant challenge but they chose grit in the face of fear or pain. That choice left a playbook for me and my kids to follow: hard work, close-knit family ties, not giving up and integrity. By comparing units of "grit measure," I have had a very easy life.

Following in the footsteps of those who walked before me, I inherited my supply of true grit, and I want to pass it on. Grit can work magic in our lives, but it's up to us to make the choice every day.

What details or lessons in this story resonate with me? And why?

How will I apply what I read or learned to my own career or personal life?

Gina
Adams

Corporate Vice President,
Government &
Regulatory Affairs
FedEx Corporation

> "Soul" is a term I like better than true grit. It evokes grace, a strength of character, a belief in doing, or at least trying to do, the right thing—always—and a knowledge or belief that some values are timeless across any culture.

> " *The daughters of lions are lions too.*"
> *- African proverb*

"Soul" is a term I like better than true grit. It evokes grace, a strength of character, a belief in doing, or at least trying to do, the right thing—always—and a knowledge or belief that some values are timeless across any culture.

I grew up in southeast Washington, D.C. By conventional measures, I was "disadvantaged:" one of eight children from a working-class family that spent time in public housing. Not unusually, my big, raucous family was touched by the criminal justice system, gun violence, substance abuse, teenage pregnancy, a lack of employment opportunities, health conditions that were treatable with health insurance, and a general lack of "access." But, it is important that you understand we had a blast growing up!

We were always encouraged to work hard, do our best and never stop dreaming. These essential lessons came from loving parents and my extended family, a few special teachers, mentors and role models. My parents were my earliest inspiration. My mother always believed — relentlessly — in work. She had a marvelous work ethic and handled money very responsibly. I never knew her to take a day off.

My father taught me confidence and perspective, sprinkled with a sense of humor. So, I learned to work very hard, manage money and never take myself too seriously.

I graduated fifth in a class of 500+ mostly Black students at Ballou High School. Although I was pretty sure I wanted to be a lawyer, I realize now that my vision of what that meant when I was younger was much smaller than what it is now. I know, for example, that any career choice can lead you in unexpected directions — and that what's most important is doing something you enjoy and doing it well.

I attended American University for undergraduate school as a Frederick Douglass scholar and then attended Howard University Law School for my J.D., where I was also on Law Review. I received my LL.M. in International and Comparative Law from Georgetown University Law Center while working full-time at my first job in the General Counsel's Office of the U.S. Department of Transportation (DOT) in the Attorney Honors Program.

A year later, I moved to the DOT's small International Law Office. There were only four or five attorneys in that office until it absorbed the Civil Aeronautics Board's international staff and grew to 14 lawyers. I was the youngest attorney and only one of four women. While I loved the job, after seven years, I realized that everyone above me was male, and white, and no one was leaving.

I decided I had to look elsewhere to advance. I'm not embarrassed to say that I had absolutely no idea how to do that. On an airplane, I had one of those woman-to-woman conversations with an industry colleague who turned out to have similar interests. Two weeks later, I got a call from FedEx and joined the company to work on regulatory matters.

During delicate negotiations with the Japanese on a bilateral aviation agreement, my boss and his wife were seriously injured in a car accident. I had to stand in and work with our General Counsel directly. I think I impressed him.

On another occasion, when I traveled with a U.S. delegation, we got to the meeting room and our host approached one of the men in the U.S. delegation and said, pointing to me, "Your assistant can sit in that corner." As you might imagine, I was not happy and I did not sit in the corner. But, I learned a few useful lessons about the world and work — and found a couple of pairs of shoes to die for.

In the 1990s, FedEx set out to transform itself from essentially an air cargo company to an integrated full-service express delivery company. After a holding company was formed, most of the lawyers went to FedEx Express, but the General Counsel chose me to work with him at corporate headquarters. Three years later, I became the company's top lobbyist.

This job has taken me places and provided experiences that I never would have imagined. For example, I've met five U.S. Presidents, world leaders, iconic entertainers, athletes — and Oprah! I've lived out of a suitcase in Asia for 30 days non-stop, visiting 11 countries and I once had one of the first cellphones in the company, about the size of a shoe box.

I still remember my first visit to the White House. I couldn't believe I was really there! The history within the walls is fascinating. Even in the restroom there was a side table with a perfect stack of disposable paper hand towels with the White House logo embedded on them. It was a keepsake I tucked into my purse to share with my proud mother. I knew this was a souvenir she would treasure.

I was also privileged to work food lines after Hurricane Katrina, teach special education classes at public schools and volunteer at homeless shelters and food banks in Washington, D.C., all in support of the FedEx Cares program. My husband of 25 years has been my biggest fan and supporter. He always encourages me to do what I love. He values my success as much as his own and has never felt threatened by my goals, my drive or my accomplishments. He encourages me to take risks, stands by me when things don't go my way and is my biggest cheerleader when they do.

We were married on a cold February day in front of over 300 family and friends. After the celebration was over, we went shopping at a department store to buy me a light jacket that I would need the next day when I boarded a plane to China. He understood that the honeymoon would have to wait. It began a loving life partnership.

The arrival of our son, Spenser, was a joy despite being months earlier than planned. Born at 28 weeks, weighing only 2 lbs., 5 oz., he was the tiniest baby I had ever seen. The first two months of his life he had to stay in the hospital to grow strong enough to go home. I passed those weeks working at the office during the day and visiting him at night. I saved my maternity leave to when I could spend all day holding him in our home.

Now that he's a tall, healthy college student at home because of the pandemic, we try to do things that expand his horizons about our family's rich history and life in general. Spenser on the other hand, does his best to keep his parents on top of the latest trends and Gen Z thinking. These lively discussions usually happen in the kitchen over a home-cooked meal. I love to cook and could have been a chef in another life. Therefore, at my home, you need to pull up a chair because conversations over food will begin. We love sports, particularly basketball, football and tennis and spend a lot of time debating who's better — LeBron, Michael Jordan or our nephew Malcolm Brogdon.

My job is all consuming. It's not an exaggeration to say I'm on call 24/7. I can't recall a vacation, or even a family matter, where work wasn't lurking in the shadows. Some say that D.C. is a rat race, filled with power lunches, relationship building dinners and fundraising galas, but there's nothing I'd change.

I live for — and crave — a good challenge! The days aren't easy. The issues are complex and there is a lot on the line in the decisions that are made.

When you have the access and ability, you should pay it forward.

When I reflect upon my journey, there have been some things I have learned that may be helpful to others. I believe that when you have the access and ability, you should pay it forward. Here are those I would like to share:

- **Work hard, but better yet, work smart.**
  Prepare for what you want by planning ahead, but not so far that you miss today.

- **Take chances.**
  Put something on the line. As former First Lady Eleanor Roosevelt said, "Do one thing every day that scares you."

- **Measure success in tiny increments.**
  Embrace the dignity in all work.

- **Understand that real self-esteem comes from achievement.**
  It isn't something you get from talk shows, self-help books or other people. Every time you do something you didn't think you could, your sense of self grows.

- **Do not become distracted by the prejudices of others.**
  Let that be THEIR problem. Your race, ethnicity and gender are not obstacles. They are simply facts of life — not excuses to do anything less than your best.

- **Keep balance and spirituality in your life.**
  Learn to forgive yourself when necessary.

- **Find the humor in life.**
  Always be able to laugh at yourself.

- **Use great care in communicating with others.**
  Proverbs, Chapter 18, Verse 21 says "death and life are in the power of the tongue." The negative language that slips into our everyday usage in this age of words and images is extremely destructive.

- **Help others.**
  If we're to survive in our communities, our societies, or even as a world — we must pay our debts forward.

- **Above all, remember that people are our most important resource.**
  Even in our technological society, treat them well and respectfully — always!

Although much progress toward racial and gender equality has been achieved socially, politically and economically, there is still much to be done here in the U.S. and abroad. I believe the collective efforts of well-intentioned people everywhere can be a beacon, an education tool, a political statement, and a rallying point for others.

Recognizing that half the population of the world are women, I am naturally interested in, and involved with, issues that affect my gender and, of course, my race. There is no doubt that education is both the common denominator and the fulcrum for the good. I say this only because my own background is not unlike that of many other people we should always be trying to reach — I know what it feels like to fight your own perceptions and those of others that suggest you're not quite — shall we say? — "worthy." But I also know the value of discipline, hard work and people who take a genuine interest in you.

I have been blessed in life beyond my wildest dreams and I understand the importance of paying that forward. I look for opportunities to be a mentor and model the way. If I can help someone look at his or her background or experiences differently and appreciate the value of lifelong learning — it means they are looking at themselves differently too.

> **Look for opportunities to be a mentor and model the way.**

I cannot tell you how strongly I believe that education — in its purest sense—is the only thing that can free us all. Women's issues — and those involving people of color — are ultimately human issues that must be fully embraced everywhere they are not; otherwise, the consequences are tragic and self-limiting. I want more — and much better — for all of us.

What details or lessons in this story resonate with me? And why?

How will I apply what I read or learned to my own career or personal life?

Karen Reddington

Regional President, Europe, FedEx Express and CEO, TNT

> Grit is when you have some fear of a particular situation, but you go ahead and do it anyway.

" *You do your best, and you can do no more* "
- Jimmy Reddington

My title at FedEx might sound a bit highfalutin, but I really don't feel that way. I have simply done what my father always told me: I have given my best. Sometimes it took grit to overcome fears or stereotypes, perseverance in challenges or sometimes long hours. But even today, that simple advice works.

I had a wonderful childhood with lots of love. I grew up in a market town in northern England. I was also an only child, which helped me be more self-sufficient, make friends and deal with tough things when they came my way. Thanks in great part to my parents, home was always my sanctuary. But like any child, life wasn't without its challenges. My mum had bouts of depression, which not only taught me grace and patience, but also the ability to cope with hard things even at an early age. My mum and dad taught me how to look for solutions to whatever life brought our way, not just stand by and worry about them. They instilled a strong determination and it has helped me to embrace grit by facing whatever challenges come my way, by moving forward even when I was afraid. And I have never shied away from a challenge or adventure since!

Even though I was an only child, I have always thought that I had a big family. My mum was one of 11 children, and I believe I was simply an extension of her siblings. My dad was one of six children. Family gatherings in Ireland in the summer were huge affairs to which I looked forward.

As a young girl in secondary school, then later in college, I became known as the "math girl." I was always drawn to math, physics and the sciences. I attended university in London to be able to experience the big city. That was my first big act of courage. While in college, I met my husband,

Angus Maxwell, who is a geologist. He was working for an engineering firm when one day, he came home and asked me, "How would you fancy living in Hong Kong for a couple of years?" I had never even traveled out of Europe, but for some reason — having never contemplated living outside of the U.K. — I immediately said, "Yes." So, we packed our bags and moved over 5,000 miles away.

Like many things in life, our opportunity was greater than our fears. I did not have a job in Hong Kong, and the only company I knew there was the airline, Cathay Pacific. I wrote them a letter which led to a job offer. While working there, I met people from FedEx. Through those relationships, I landed an even better job as a business adviser with FedEx's planning and engineering department.

I quickly realized in my new position that I was in a male dominated world. Many women do not pursue education or careers in STEM, but it doesn't have to be that way. With a PhD in Operations Research and work experience in the field, I have a strong message of empowerment for women who are drawn to math, science and engineering. I am active in sharing career paths and opportunities in STEM with women around the world. And, I encourage the same about pursuing a career with a logistics company, like FedEx. There are so many examples of great women who have wonderful and fulfilling careers.

We have two daughters, both now young adults. Both are strong academically and they are both inclined toward being "math girls." I cherish family time with our girls. We love travel, cooking and being together as a family. Before trips, I enjoy reading about the places and people we plan to visit so we can get the most out of our trip, while they tend to enjoy lounging on the beach!

Of course, there are times in my career that the demands of the job create a challenge with work-life balance. I am often required to take calls late into the evenings because of my responsibilities across multiple time zones. But I have learned to be intentional about that balance, manage around the business calls and try to be available for what my family needs. My girls knew that a question about homework or simply wanting to tell me 'good night' one more time could interrupt any call.

There are still some trade-offs, but I have learned to prioritize and give my best to both work and family. I never really missed big school events, like plays and concerts, but I was never usually able to pick them up at the school gate in the afternoons. I do remember one time when I did go to pick up my youngest daughter from school. When she saw me, she screamed, "Mummy!" dropped her book bag and sprinted toward me to jump into my arms. My friend, who witnessed it, told me with tears in her eyes that it was the sweetest thing she had ever seen.

As the girls get older, they appreciate my need to work and understand why it took so much time away from them. But that understanding got severely tested when they were 11 and 13 years old when we moved from Hong Kong to Singapore for a promotion. Things were going just fine when, several years later, I was offered another wonderful promotion that would require a move back to Hong Kong. I did not want to uproot the family again. My husband is a fantastic father. He had a strong mother and two sisters, and I believe that helped him better understand women. So, thanks to Angus, we worked through the decision on whether I should take the promotion. He readily agreed to remain in Singapore with the girls while I commuted between Hong Kong and Singapore for two years. He did all this whilst continuing to run his own business, but he was willing to make the sacrifice for me to accept the job and continue my move up the FedEx ladder.

Both my parents passed away when my girls were quite young. It is stunning how quickly such important people in our lives can suddenly no longer be there. My dad, Jimmy, was sitting in his favorite easy chair talking about lunch. The next minute, he was gone. I would have loved for my parents to have seen how wonderfully their granddaughters have turned out, and for the girls to have spent more time with them. I know my mum and dad would have been proud of them, and of what I have accomplished in my professional life.

I never imagined I would be where I am today in my career. The young me, back in the small town in northern England, would have been terrified by being in such a large and important position with such a major company. People assume I am ambitious. No, not really. I am curious. I ask a lot of questions and am not afraid of challenging the status quo if I see there are ways to make things better for our customers or for our team members.

I have benefited significantly in my career by strong mentors and other leaders at FedEx who believed in me, challenged and offered advice. I had a boss in planning and engineering who kept giving me extra work. She saw more in me than I saw in myself. She pushed me out of my comfort zone. She told me she saw that I had the capacity to do more.

Success is built on authenticity, bringing the "real you" to everything you do.

I also learned that success is built on authenticity, bringing the "real you" to everything you do. At FedEx, we value people and support individual strengths that allow team members to contribute uniquely and as a team. FedEx nurtures diversity and authenticity in the workforce. I am a happy and positive person and have always chosen to look more for brightness rather than dwelling on darkness. That is not what some expect from someone in my position, but that is who I am. I strive to be approachable and relatable, and I am concise about making decisions. When opportunities present themselves, I typically ask, "How will I feel if I don't do this?" That helps make the decision.

So many things are out of our control, but our reactions to them are fully in our court. I am a person who lives with epilepsy. With the help of doctors, I can control the condition with medication. I can't just make the epilepsy go away, but I can control whether I let it define me or what I am capable of accomplishing. My approach is what I learned as a child: take control of what I can and push on. I've even been spotted riding a bicycle around my new city of Amsterdam. Even though I'm somewhat of a liability to myself, I am determined to get on that bike!

I am especially proud of my former team in Asia and my new team in Europe. The FedEx team from China is a terrific example of "who we are and what we do." When they first heard about the COVID-19 outbreak, the anxiety level was intense, but they recognized the need to start immediately implementing health and safety measures for our 1,000 team members in Wuhan, capital of Hubei, China. The team understood that COVID-19 would not be a typical business crisis related to weather or international trade issues. This crisis required an entirely new playbook and swift decision making that dealt with global uncertainty and the emotional and personal impacts of our team members and customers. We had to react as we received information and guidance from the government. That required out-of-the-box thinking and a strong reliance on experience. It is a great source of pride when we see such a challenge not as something impossible to overcome but as a wonderful opportunity to shine. And shine they did.

So many things are out of our control but our reactions to them are fully in our court.

I was recently taking a walk through my new home city of Amsterdam when I felt a strong sense of déjà vu. The first time I had been in this city was way back when, as a PhD candidate, I came here to present a research paper I had authored. I was nervous since it was my first time to present to such a large group of people. I wore my only best dress, which likely made me look even younger and smaller than I was. But as my parents had taught me, I summoned up the grit, faced my fears and pushed through. Afterward, a professor who had been in the audience came up to me and said, "Young lady, that certainly was a lot of work for a little girl." I wasn't too enamored with being called a little girl, but as I strolled through this beautiful city 30 years on, it struck me that this small-town girl that had given that presentation had now come full circle.

It has certainly been a lot of work for a little girl.

What details or lessons in this story resonate with me? And why?

How will I apply what I read or learned to my own career or personal life?

> *"This too shall pass."*
> *- Abraham Lincoln*

Aimee DiCicco-Ruhl

Senior Vice President, Sales
FedEx Office

At the age of 35, my grandmother Nunni was diagnosed with breast cancer. Everyone in the family was scared to death. In 1956, people knew little about breast cancer and treatments for the disease were rough and debilitating. Besides that, her doctors were not confident about her possibilities for surviving.

But my grandmother set an amazing example in her fight with cancer. She did not hide her experience from anyone. Though she underwent a mastectomy — her entire right side was just rib cage and scar tissue — she never showed fear or shame, at least that anyone around her could see. She remained the beautiful, strong woman she always had been and even kept that sense of humor that all admired. And cancer was not the only health issue she faced. To be honest, her challenges would have stopped most people in their tracks but not my grandmother.

Nunni maintained that Jesus had answered her prayers and allowed her to live because He had more things for her to do. She was relentless with each challenge that came her way. As her life progressed, severe degenerative arthritis set in. If her pain got too bad, she would take the least drastic pain medication she had, sit down and be still for 30 minutes, then carry on. She said she was allowing the pills to "take the edge off," and then she would go make a pie or take a walk or even help others. She didn't quit, she didn't engage in self-pity. She kept moving in faith.

My Nunni was the first person I knew who had "made it to the other side" — she made it through a potentially fatal situation and came out stronger than ever. I had no idea that watching her example would help me later in life, at a time when I needed it the most.

> True grit fuels us to keep on going, no matter how difficult the situation may be. Grit allows us to push through tough situations, knowing what grounds you, what your true north is and believing there is always another side.

My childhood is like a collection of chapters in a book that all tie together in the end. But each section seems to be 180 degrees different than the one before it.

Early on, my life seemed perfect. Although I only had one sibling — a brother six years younger — we had a large extended Italian family, who all lived close-by in our Pennsylvania neighborhood. From birth I lived next door to my paternal great-grandparents, and I spent as much time there as I did in my own home, finding the blend of English and Italian a normal cadence. At Nunni's and Pap's, my maternal grandparents, we all came together once a week for a huge meal and plenty of loud conversation and fun.

When I was very young, my great-grandfather introduced me to great literature and instilled my love of reading. He read to me every morning after grandma and I made his breakfast. All the grandchildren were exposed to the beauty of classical music because my paternal grandmother played piano and entertained us with the works of the great composers. It was a wonderful atmosphere in which to grow up, with lots of people our age to play with and plenty of love to go around. The chapter in my early childhood years was almost perfect, but that changed quickly.

My dad came out of the Navy with welding skills and promptly became a millworker, but he was wired to be an entrepreneur. That was just one of the traits I inherited from him. He soon moved from welding to starting his own businesses: a restaurant, a painting company and more. The restaurant became a big success and a central gathering place for all generations in our little town. But like many of us in life, he also made some bad choices that led to tremendous emotional strain on my mother and our family. This next chapter in my life was completely different from the first as our family situation went from high tide to hitting rock bottom.

I was in the fourth grade when things began to deteriorate in my life. I was perceptive beyond my years and aware of strain in my family relationships and the emotional and financial devastation that resulted. It was in this period that I quickly learned how to navigate through tense situations. I became resourceful, doing what had to be done to try to restore harmony in our home. I also became a negotiator, finding ways to spend as much time as possible away from home with my Nunni and Pap. They were my anchor in childhood and reminders of more carefree times. But I couldn't escape the problems entirely. In a small town, everyone knows your business. As years progressed and not-so-kind comments were made by schoolmates or by teachers and friends' parents, I made it my goal not to let anyone see I was upset. I believed they would use those signs of weakness against me or feel sorry for me.

Life was hard. But in the worst of it, there were still laughs with cousins at gatherings and Sunday dinners with grandparents. Somehow, there was always food. Even when we had no money for oil to heat our home, my mother found a way to put dinner on the table. Our Nunni and Pap's home was my refuge, just as good as any theme park or playground. They were an escape from some very harsh realities. Thanks to a love of music, books and dance, I found escape and discovered some things about my own strengths. I was creative, appreciated the beauty of music and words coming together. I loved performing, losing myself on the stage in front of an audience of any size.

We eventually lost our home and the restaurant and moved in with my mom's parents. If people didn't know how bad it was to that point, they did then. In a pivotal time, I made a decision not to be embarrassed about my situation. It was difficult for a young child to do, but I held my head high and simply pushed through it, just the way my grandmother had done, persevering and ultimately beating breast cancer.

In one of the most valuable life lessons of redemption, my dad eventually hit rock bottom. This stopped the downward spiral we were all caught up in. He got back up, repented, and began rebuilding his marriage and our lives. He truly became a changed man. And in an equally valuable lesson, my mother forgave and made the choice to move forward. All was not perfect; we were still destitute in terms of material possessions, but we still had each other, life's most valuable gifts. My father took a construction job and little by little got us back on track. Answering that entrepreneurial inner voice, he started a painting contracting company. By the time I left for college my family was able to move into our own home again. So, I had started yet another chapter, one in which my situation changed for the better.

Through it all, I knew I was loved despite the heartache and trials. I witnessed firsthand that all choices have consequences — and they impact others for better or worse. But those choices can also change. No situation is ever too bad or too far gone to be redeemed. Do not ever tell me a person cannot change. My parents are financially secure, the world's best grandparents, celebrated their 55th wedding anniversary and remain lovebirds.

I can thank my dad for my first job out of college. Like many new grads, I found myself over-educated but, with no experience, under-qualified for most positions I sought. One day my dad was working on one of his painting jobs when he struck up a conversation with an executive coming out of the building. Dad asked him if his company was hiring. He said that they did have some openings. "Hire my daughter, then," Dad told him. After a few interviews, they did.

I signed on as a customer service agent with Roadway Package System (RPS), which is now FedEx Ground. That was when I put into use some of those lessons I had learned during the dark years. I had a positive attitude and a strong work ethic. From the earliest days with my extended family, I was comfortable with communicating and selling ideas, so a promotion into sales was a natural fit. I credit my big, gregarious, say-what-you-mean-and-mean-what-you-say family for helping me break through into a male-dominated field. I simply ignored being told what wasn't possible and did not let naysayers bother me at all.

I loved working at FedEx from the very beginning, for three reasons. First, FedEx measures worth based on skill. Who you know, where you came from and how much money you have do not matter to the company. FedEx is interested in what you can do and how well you do it. Second, team members are the top priority, and FedEx operates very much like one big family — like mine. Like my big Italian family, the company has always been there for me when I needed them the most.

Finally, I met my husband, Craig, on my very first day on the job. He has always been my biggest champion and stood by me through some truly tough times.

Ours has always been a partnership of give and take. He is also in sales, a naturally competitive area, but he was perfectly willing to pull back his career growth so he could be with our two boys while I did the late hours, hard days, and travel required for advancement. He looked me in the eye and told me, "My money is on you when it comes to which one of us has the most upward mobility potential." I am grateful for that belief and support.

Now here I am, 28 years with FedEx, still amazed at how far I have come, the experiences I have had, places I have been and the people I have met along the way. In many ways I consider myself the "accidental executive."

The book of my life has many more chapters now, with ups and downs — some darker than I'd imagined. As unpleasant as they were, those challenges shaped me, made me stronger and became valuable life lessons as the next chapters unfolded. Sales involves resourcefulness, negotiating skills, perceptivity and coming from a position of strength.

And personally, little did I know just how much I would one day need the example set by my grandmother as a breast cancer survivor. Just before my 31st birthday, while getting dressed for dinner one night, I noticed a marble-sized lump in my right breast. My first reaction was to assume it was nothing so I could keep the fear from derailing my emotions. A mammogram and pathology report proved me wrong. I had an aggressive form of breast cancer. When my family heard the news, they cranked up a phone chain and helped me make crucial decisions about where I would have my treatment. My father even asked my surgeon if he was willing to treat me just as he would his own daughter. He also insisted on speaking with an oncologist about whether I would have to have chemotherapy afterward and exactly what kind it would be. I wanted to know everything about my fight. That has always been the way I attacked any problem in life. Get the facts, pray and forge ahead.

Forging ahead was no cake walk. I was sick much of the time, lost my hair and fingernails and suffered intense bone pain. But it was worth it. Bad as it was, the treatment worked. I have been cancer-free for 17 years. And through it all, my family never left my side. For the entire time I was being treated, I never once cried. But the day my oncologist told me the disease was gone, that I was cancer-free 10 years later, I sobbed in gratitude and relief.

I was blessed that my grandmother was still living and could celebrate the end of treatment with me. She passed prior to that 10-year appointment, but I know she was also just as proud of me as I was of her.

I haven't forgotten the gratitude of that 10-year appointment and have harnessed it to help others in any way I can. I have made it a mission to dedicate time in support of other women going through breast cancer diagnoses and treatment. I am a former national board member for Susan G. Komen for the Cure. I only wish I could wrap my arms around every woman facing this disease so I could let them know that they are not alone. Not everyone has such excellent medical care as I received or is blessed with such a helpful family. But I want them to know that they can get through this and that there is love and support out there for them.

Just when Craig and I thought things could not get any better, we were blessed — twice! Because of all the chemotherapy, and because I was not that far away from turning 40-years old, my husband and I assumed we would never be able to have children because of my type of cancer and associated complications. But then a true miracle happened in our lives when we found out we were pregnant with our first child! Though it was a high-risk pregnancy, and doctors were worried about complications and potential problems with the baby, Jonah was absolutely perfect. Next, because God probably knew that people would doubt the first miracle, I was pregnant again within six months, and Noah came into this world just as picture-perfect as his big brother. I call him the exclamation point on God's plan. This was my favorite chapter in the book of life yet.

Through it all, I still wasn't prepared for the fact that there might be yet another dark chapter in my story. But, there was. My husband was diagnosed with a rare cancer, one so aggressive and deadly that we had to leave our toddlers behind with non-family members while we went to MD Anderson Cancer Center in Houston in search of a treatment. We were blessed that one of the world's preeminent experts on Sarcoma — and one of only two with expertise in Craig's rare cancer — was there. There is no treatment protocol because there is only a 7% two-year survival rate, and only 11 people in the world are diagnosed every year. But this doctor gave us a shot at a treatment that had as much chance of killing Craig as saving him. We prayerfully and gratefully took that chance. It took most of the year and precious time away from our babies requiring both of us to put our careers aside. It was something I wouldn't wish on my worst enemy, but in the end, Craig made a miraculous recovery. As of now, he is six years cancer-free.

In addition to being able to help breast cancer patients and survivors, I could now talk to and help others facing battles with all forms of cancer. Cancer seems to keep finding me — in addition to my grandmother, many others in the family have suffered and fought the battle, not always winning — but it also opens even more opportunities for me to help others.

So what are the foundations that have guided me throughout the highs and lows of my life book so far?

Faith
I am a very spiritual woman. Faith and family are the two biggest things in my life. I start each day very early with a cup of coffee, my Bible and some worship music.

Exercise
I take time for exercise. I am a proponent of movement and body connectivity. I exercise every day for 45 minutes to an hour. That gets me physically and mentally ready for the day.

Gratitude
I make sure I hug the kids as often as they allow, and then a little more.

Authentic Caring
We can inherit both good and bad things. My mother is warm, compassionate, the kind of person everyone dreams of for a mom. My dad is much more direct and

does not hesitate to tell people what they need to do to get things done. Be tough. Talk in a way that some might consider harsh, hard, direct, but tell people what they need to hear — even "No!" He believes you are doing a person a favor, empowering them, when you are direct and determined. I am more like him in that regard. But even when I am so direct, I borrow some of that "authentic caring" I inherited from my mom and speak truth in kindness in a way that helps me connect on a personal level.

Tough talk. Tough love.

I remember one especially wonderful example of being on the receiving end of that kind of encouragement. We had one of our big sales meetings during the last of my chemo treatments. I decided I would go, even though I did not feel well, had lost all my hair and did not want anyone feeling sorry for me. I chose to wear a particularly bright-red bandanna for the opening session that morning. A senior leader of our sales team stepped to the podium to welcome us all. He has always been a big supporter and booster of mine. That day, the first thing he did was point me out and compliment me on my beautiful, bright-red bandanna. That could have been a bad thing, an embarrassing thing, coming from anyone else, or said in a different way. But that was his way of letting me know everyone was on my side, that I was loved. And it had the precise effect he was going for. The resulting applause and smiles were amazingly therapeutic.

We all have grit inside, we just have to make the decision to tap it and not give up.

True grit fuels us to keep on going, no matter how difficult the situation may be. Grit allows us to push through tough situations, knowing what grounds you, what your true north is and believing there is always another side. For me that means admitting something is hard and fighting along with a commitment to prayer, to live, to love, to find joy, even as you go through something that seems impossible. We all have the grit inside, we just have to make the decision to tap it and not give up.

So, what chapters lie ahead? I have no way of knowing. But I do know that I am armed with what I need to face the inevitable challenges — faith, family, friends, our team at FedEx — and that means that I am confident and ready to face the next chapters of my life.

What details or lessons in this story resonate with me? And why?

How will I apply what I read or learned to my own career or personal life?

About the Book-Edie Hand's Closing Comments

When I first began telling the stories of extraordinary, strong women who had great life experiences or those who overcame all sorts of setbacks and challenges to find success — and used those qualities and success to serve others — I decided that I needed a one or two word description for what they had in common. Then it came to me. And it was a word I had heard since I was a little girl, growing up in rural Northwest Alabama.

The word was "grit," sometimes modified to include "true grit."

It came from my precious grandmother, Alice Hood Hacker. She was my mom's mom and we always called her "Grandma Alice."

I have always had a pretty good idea of what the term "true grit" means to me. However, when I decided to tell the stories of those women who seemed to personify every aspect of the concept, I knew I would have to confirm how each of them defined grit. Every one of them certainly had true grit, at least by my definition. I was not surprised that most of them mentioned the same words, "perseverance," "strong will," "tenacity," and "pushing through to get done what has to be done" when they told me their definitions of grit.

Grandma Alice always told us we had the power to do hard things if we only had the will and the grit. She also taught me the value of food, faith, friends and family to help get us through those rough patches on life's road. As a child, I had no idea how much I would need all of those things or just how rocky that road would be.

We were not wealthy but lived very comfortably, growing up in the community of Burnout, Alabama. I was the oldest, with three younger brothers, and, much later, a sister. My dad seemed to be working all the time, trying to put food on the table and make a success of his various businesses. My mother was often ill. We called it "bad nerves" back in those days, but it was severe migraine headaches and depression, a condition hardly understood then. So, it fell on me to help raise my brothers. Even at 12-years-old, I was performing adult chores and taking on grown-up responsibilities. I don't remember much time at all just being a little girl.

But there were absolutely some good times. We were blessed to live on a farm and to have access to a barn, forty acres of pastureland, and our cherished horses. My brothers, Terry, David, and Phillip Blackburn, and I would ride them and talk about our ambitions. For me, many of those aspirations came from seeing how others in our very musical family loved to perform. There were some gifted singers and songwriters that included my cousin, Elvis Presley. I was fortunate to be able to take piano lessons and enjoyed playing for my family on special occasions.

I loved my brothers so much and fully expected to grow old with them. It was not to be. David died in an automobile accident when he was 19 years old, when he and I were both in college. Ten years later, Phillip also died in a car wreck. And 15 years after that, Terry had an aneurysm in the brain that left him virtually helpless, even though his mind was fine. For the next five years, my mother, sister, and I cared for him until he ultimately lost the battle.

As each one of these tragedies hit us, I could hear Grandma Alice whispering in my ear, reminding us about how we sometimes had to do hard things. As she had taught me, I relied on faith, family, and friends as never before to get me through each of these heartbreaking losses. Grit served me well.

As it turned out, I did get to live out many of my dreams. I went to New York where I did some work with the CBS television affiliate there and had a recurring role on the long-running television drama "As the World Turns." But because of the losses in my family, I ultimately chose to come back south. Before long, I met Lincoln Hand, who would become my husband and father of our son, Linc, the light of my life.

Once back home in Alabama, I still had many things I wanted to accomplish. I soon opened an advertising agency and found success helping build both local and national campaigns for clients. Some had me back in front of the camera, too. My work also included a great deal of writing commercials. That led to yet another aspect of my career: writing books, telling stories, and speaking.

We never know what hard things we may be called upon to do in our lives, or just how tenacious we may have to be just to get through them. I have also had to face one of the most dreaded medical diagnoses there is — cancer — and do so multiple times. These experiences certainly taught me the value of perseverance.

Each time I got the test results and the bad news, I relied not only on the words of Grandma Alice, but also on that true grit I felt I inherited from her. I have always thought of her words, reminding me of how a pearl starts as a single grain of sand. Over time, that tiny bit of grit becomes a beautiful jewel. Beautiful and tough. So far, it has worked. I have bounced back each time I faced cancer and emerged even stronger than before.

That is one reason I am so proud to be able to bring stories of exceptional women to a wider audience as "women of true grit," so others can see how it is done. These women are powerful role models, mentors, examples of what can be done if we simply do not allow life's rough patches to derail and defeat us.

Some of us spend too much time looking back. Or, because hindsight is always 20/20, we judge ourselves too harshly. That is not productive at all. We all have to forgive ourselves for the wrong choices we may have made. We have to realize that we always did what we thought was right and, hopefully, did not surrender easily.

I am convinced that grit is something we are all born with. It is such a waste when we don't use it to do remarkable things that we may have doubted we could ever do. It is crucial we develop the confidence to call upon it when we need it, the knowledge to know how to apply it to whatever the obstacle might be, and the courage to carry on to do those hard things, no matter how impossible that might appear to be at the time.

That is what these women of true grit have done. I hope their stories — and mine — will help others overcome challenges, achieve their biggest goals, and live every dream in every season of life.

Edie Hand

About the Author

Edie Hand is a businesswoman, speaker, media personality, filmmaker, author and mom. She has authored or been a part of authoring over 25 books.

The Edie Hand Foundation's brand "Women of True Grit" encourages women to share their stories and passion from the trials they face to their triumphs.

WOMEN OF TRUE GRIT®

Edie has starred in national commercials, daytime television soaps, hosted national TV, and developed several radio shows and vignettes across the country. She was the CEO of a full-service ad company, Hand 'N Hand Advertising, in Birmingham and Daphne, Alabama for over 30 years. In recent years she partnered with her Hollywood actor/businessman son, Linc Hand, to form Hand 'N Hand Entertainment to continue her writing for film, television, radio, and podcasts.

Edie is a numerous time cancer survivor and understands living with chronic illness but always finds the grit to keep moving onward and upward. She learned how to turn hard things into beautiful situations.

She also comes from a wonderful family heritage of songwriting, acting, and music from the Hood-Hacker-Presley Family. Her legendary cousin was Elvis Presley where she learned first-hand about paying life forward through charities in One's community.

Edie's alma mater is the University of North Alabama and she resides near Birmingham, Alabama.

To learn more about Edie, her books, the charities she supports and her speaking topics visit www.ediehand.com

About the Author

Jane

Amaba

Jane Amaba is a wife, mother and vice president of finance at FedEx Services. Her team provides analysis and actionable financial guidance to facilitate corporate prioritization of strategic projects.

Jane is the executive sponsor of the Women in Leadership Business Resource Team at FedEx Services with a mission to engage, enrich, empower and elevate women at FedEx. She is a three time FedEx Five star winner, the corporation's highest honor, and an ASQ certified QDM Expert.

She is a member of the National Leadership Council for CureJM.org, a non-profit organization founded to raise the awareness, and support for finding a cure, for juvenile dermatomyositis, a rare and life-threatening auto-immune disease.

Jane previously served on the Board for Girls Inc. Memphis, inspiring girls to be strong, smart and bold, and on the Foundation Board for LeBonheur Children's hospital in Memphis, which is consistently ranked as one of the nation's top children's hospitals by US News and World Reports.

She served as vice-chair of the United Way's Women's Leadership Giving program and is a member of the United Way's Alexis de Tocqueville Society. She has served on the City of Doral Citizen's Audit Board, during her tenure with FedEx Express in the Latin American and Caribbean Division, headquartered in Miami, Florida.

Jane holds an MBA from the University of Georgia and a bachelor's of science in finance, from Virginia Polytechnic Institute and State University. She also holds a Certificate of Professional Development from the Wharton School of Business at the University of Pennsylvania and a Certificate of Executive Women in Leadership from Cornell University.